Collins
COBUILD

Key Words for
Mechanical
Engineering

HarperCollins Publishers
Westerhill Road
Bishopbriggs
Glasgow
G64 2QT

First Edition 2013

Reprint 10 9 8 7 6 5 4 3 2 1 0

© HarperCollins Publishers 2013

ISBN 978-0-00-748978-7

Collins® and COBUILD® are
registered trademarks of
HarperCollins Publishers Limited

www.collinslanguage.com

A catalogue record for this book is
available from the British Library

CD recorded by Networks SRL,
Milan, Italy

Typeset by Davidson Publishing
Solutions, Glasgow

Printed in Great Britain by Clays Ltd,
St Ives plc

Acknowledgements

We would like to thank those authors
and publishers who kindly gave
permission for copyright material
to be used in the Collins Corpus.
We would also like to thank Times
Newspapers Ltd for providing
valuable data.

HarperCollins does not warrant
that www.collinsdictionary.com,
www.collinslanguage.com or any
other website mentioned in this title
will be provided uninterrupted, that
any website will be error free, that
defects will be corrected, or that the
website or the server that makes it
available are free of viruses or bugs.
For full terms and conditions please
refer to the site terms provided on
the website.

Contents

Contributors

Specialist consultant
Professor Bob Reuben, Institute of Mechanical, Process and Energy
Engineering, School of Engineering and Physical Sciences,
Heriot-Watt University

Project manager
Patrick White

Editors
Katherine Carroll
Gavin Gray
Justin Nash
Ruth O'Donovan
Enid Pearsons
Elizabeth Walter
Laura Wedgeworth
Kate Woodford

Computing support
Mark Taylor

For the publisher
Gerry Breslin
Lucy Cooper
Kerry Ferguson
Elaine Higgleton
Rosie Pearce
Lisa Sutherland

Introduction

Collins COBUILD Key Words for Mechanical Engineering is a brand-new vocabulary book for students who want to master the English of Mechanical Engineering in order to study or work in the field. This title contains the 500 most important English words and phrases relating to Mechanical Engineering, as well as a range of additional features which have been specially designed to help you to *really* understand and use the language of this specific area.

The main body of the book contains alphabetically organized dictionary-style entries for the key words and phrases of Mechanical Engineering. These vocabulary items have been specially chosen to fully prepare you for the type of language that you will need in this field. Many are specialized terms that are very specific to this profession and area of study. Others are more common or general words and phrases that are often used in the context of Mechanical Engineering.

Each word and phrase is explained clearly and precisely, in English that is easy to understand. In addition, each entry is illustrated with examples taken from the Collins Corpus. Of course, you will also find grammatical information about the way that the words and phrases behave.

In amongst the alphabetically organized entries, you will find valuable word-building features that will help you gain a better understanding of this area of English. For example, some features provide extra help with tricky pronunciations, while others pull together groups of related words that can usefully be learned as a set.

At the start of this book you will see lists of words and phrases, helpfully organized by topic area. You can use these lists to revise sets of vocabulary and to prepare for writing tasks. You will also find with this book an MP3 CD, containing a recording of each headword in the book, followed by an example sentence. This will help you to learn and remember pronunciations of words and phrases. Furthermore, the exercise section at the end of this book gives you an opportunity to memorize important words and phrases, to assess what you have learned, and to work out which areas still need attention.

So whether you are studying Mechanical Engineering, or you are already working in the field and intend to improve your career prospects, we are confident that *Collins COBUILD Key Words for Mechanical Engineering* will equip you for success in the future.

Guide to Dictionary Entries

Headwords are organized in alphabetical order

Pronunciation

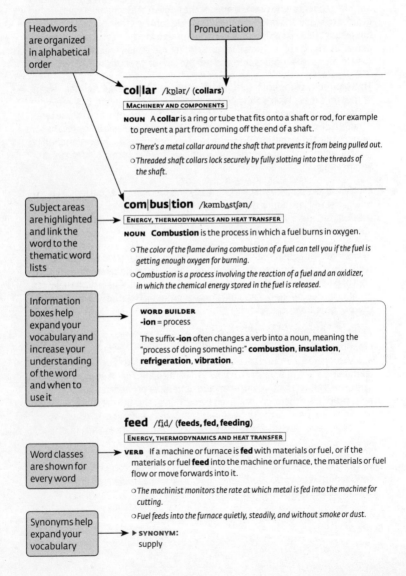

col|lar /kɒlər/ (collars)

MACHINERY AND COMPONENTS

NOUN A **collar** is a ring or tube that fits onto a shaft or rod, for example to prevent a part from coming off the end of a shaft.

○ There's a metal collar around the shaft that prevents it from being pulled out.

○ Threaded shaft collars lock securely by fully slotting into the threads of the shaft.

com|bus|tion /kəmbʌstʃən/

ENERGY, THERMODYNAMICS AND HEAT TRANSFER

NOUN **Combustion** is the process in which a fuel burns in oxygen.

○ The color of the flame during combustion of a fuel can tell you if the fuel is getting enough oxygen for burning.

○ Combustion is a process involving the reaction of a fuel and an oxidizer, in which the chemical energy stored in the fuel is released.

Subject areas are highlighted and link the word to the thematic word lists

Information boxes help expand your vocabulary and increase your understanding of the word and when to use it

> **WORD BUILDER**
> **-ion** = process
>
> The suffix **-ion** often changes a verb into a noun, meaning the "process of doing something:" **combustion**, **insulation**, **refrigeration**, **vibration**.

feed /fiːd/ (feeds, fed, feeding)

ENERGY, THERMODYNAMICS AND HEAT TRANSFER

VERB If a machine or furnace is **fed** with materials or fuel, or if the materials or fuel **feed** into the machine or furnace, the materials or fuel flow or move forwards into it.

○ The machinist monitors the rate at which metal is fed into the machine for cutting.

○ Fuel feeds into the furnace quietly, steadily, and without smoke or dust.

Word classes are shown for every word

Synonyms help expand your vocabulary

▶ SYNONYM:
supply

Guide to Dictionary Entries

Variants of the headword, such as abbreviated, full forms and British forms, are also shown

C|M|M /siː ɛm ɛm/ (short for **Coordinate Measurement Machine**)

CONTROL, INSTRUMENTATION AND METROLOGY

ABBREVIATION A **CMM** is a robot used for measuring the shape of a component by touching it repeatedly with a probe (= a long thin electronic sensing device).

Definitions explain what the word means in simple language

○ The CMM was programmed to measure the specimen at 400 different positions, thus producing a map of its shape.

○ It takes two or three days to program the CMM and run the measurements.

Examples show how the word is used in context

reg|is|ter /rɛdʒɪstər/ (**registers, registered, registering**)

MANUFACTURING AND ASSEMBLY

VERB If a mechanical part **registers**, it lines up with another.

All the different forms of the word are listed

○ When the tube is turned so that its hole registers with a second tube, fluid can flow from one tube to the other.

○ A port in the journal registers with a similar port in the bearing.

▶ **COLLOCATION:**
register with

Collocations help you put the word into practice

Guide to Pronunciation Symbols

Vowel Sounds

ɑ	calm, ah
ɑr	heart, far
æ	act, mass
ɑɪ	dive, cry
ɑɪər	fire, tire
ɑʊ	out, down
ɑʊər	flour, sour
ɛ	met, lend, pen
eɪ	say, weight
ɛər	fair, care
ɪ	fit, win
i	feed, me
ɪər	near, beard
ɒ	lot, spot
oʊ	note, coat
ɔ	claw, bought
ɔr	more, cord
ɔɪ	boy, joint
ʊ	could, stood
u	you, use
ʊər	lure, endure
ɜr	turn, third
ʌ	fund, must
ə	*the first vowel in* about
ər	*the first vowel in* forgotten
i	*the second vowel in* very
u	*the second vowel in* actual

Consonant Sounds

b	bed, rub
d	done, red
f	fit, if
g	good, dog
h	hat, horse
y	yellow, you
k	king, pick
l	lip, bill
ᵊl	handle, panel
m	mat, ram
n	not, tin
ᵊn	hidden, written
p	pay, lip
r	run, read
s	soon, bus
t	talk, bet
v	van, love
w	win, wool
w	why, wheat
z	zoo, buzz
ʃ	ship, wish
ʒ	measure, leisure
ŋ	sing, working
tʃ	cheap, witch
θ	thin, myth
ð	then, other
dʒ	joy, bridge

Word lists

CONTROL, INSTRUMENTATION AND METROLOGY

accelerometer
actuator
adaptive
anvil
artificial intelligence
caliper
CMM
control
controller bias
controller gain
control loop
cruise control
differential
display
dynamic response
end effector
error
feedback
gage
integral
interferometer
manipulator
manometer
metrology
micrometer
navigation system
non-destructive testing
orifice meter
PID
Pitot tube
proportional
proximity probe
regulate
regulator
relay
robot
sensor
setpoint
shaft encoder
stability
strain gage
thermocouple
thermometer
tuning
velocimetry

ENERGY, THERMODYNAMICS AND HEAT TRANSFER

air-conditioning
air-cool
boiling
combustion
compressor
condensation
conduction
convection
coolant
cycle
diffusion
economizer
efficiency
energy
equation of state
equilibrium
expansion
feed
fin
fission
flux
forced convection
freezing
fuel
fusion
gas turbine
geothermal energy
heat
heater
heat pump
heat transfer

insulation
irreversible
live steam
melting
natural convection
natural gas
nuclear energy
nuclear reactor
phase
photovoltaic
power
psychrometry
radiation
Rankine cycle
refrigerant
refrigeration
renewable energy
reversible
steady-state
steam boiler
steam turbine
superheating
system
temperature
thermodynamics
transient
wind turbine
work

FLUID ENGINEERING

air-intake
air turbine
atomize
atomizer
baffle
ball valve
blank
bleed
bleed valve
bypass

centrifugal pump
check valve
choke
cut-off
drag
duct
fan
fluid
gate valve
gland
head
header
hose
hydraulic
hydraulic ram
hydrostatic pressure
inlet
intake
inviscid
irrotational
laminar
lubrication
multiphase flow
needle valve
nozzle
open channel
packing
pneumatic
poppet
port
potential flow
pump
rheology
shock wave
slide valve
slug flow
static head
streamline
supersonic
turbine
turbulent
valve

valve spring
viscosity

GENERAL

acceleration
beam
billet
boiler
bolt
bracing
centrifugal force
compression
cross-section
disk
dynamics
force
friction
fulcrum
furnace
idle
impact
incompressible
ingot
instrumentation
laser
lever
male
manufacture
mechanical advantage
mechanics
metallurgy
motor
Newtonian
output
plate
pressure vessel
rod
rolling resistance
safety valve
shaft

sheet
shell
shoulder
shut-off
slab
slave
socket
spindle
spline
spring
stud
thread
throttle
tool
tooling
tooth
transmit
unit
universal joint
washer
web
wedge

MACHINERY AND COMPONENTS

axle
backlash
ball-and-socket joint
ball bearing
bayonet
bearing
belt drive
bevel gear
boss
bush
cage
cam
camshaft
carriage
chain drive
clutch

cog
coil spring
collar
connecting rod
control
coupler
coupling
crank
crankcase
crankshaft
crosshead
cylinder
dashpot
dead center
differential
displacement
drum
engine
exhaust
eyebolt
finger
fishplate
fitting
flange
floating
flywheel
follower
friction clutch
gasket
gear
gearing
governor
grab
grommet
guide
helical gear
hinge
housing
hub
hunt
jacket
journal

keyway
knuckle joint
liner
link
linkage
locknut
master cylinder
mechanism
mesh
nut
pawl
pivot
rack-and-pinion
ram
ratchet
rocker
roller bearing
rolling bearing
screw
seal
self-tapping
sleeve
sprocket
spur gear
sump
tappet
thrust bearing
wing nut
worm gear
wrist pin

MANUFACTURING AND ASSEMBLY

annealing
arbor
assembly
assembly line
bed
bit
blank

blow molding
bore
boring
burr
CAD system
casting
center
chatter
chip
chuck
CNC
cold shut
cold working
computer-aided process planning
cushion
cutting tool
die
die casting
draw
drilling
eccentricity
extrusion
faceplate
feeder
fixture
flash
flexible assembly system
flute
forging
forming
grinding
grinding wheel
ground
guillotine
gun
honing
hopper
hot working
hydraulic press
index
investment casting
jaw

jig
kinematics
laser machining
lathe
layup
machinability
machine
machine tool
machining
mandrel
mill
milling
milling machine
molding
normalizing
open-die forging
pack
pilot
porosity
press
pultrusion
quality assurance
quality system
rake angle
rapid prototyping
reaming
register
relief angle
relieved
riser
robot arm
runner
sand casting
screw
shielded metal arc welding
shim
shrinkage
slag
solid model
spot weld
spot-weld
statistical process control

stereolithography
stress relief
surface treatment
tap
tolerance
turning
vacuum molding
weldability
welding
workability
workpiece

MATERIALS

adhesive
alloy
brittle
carbon steel
cast iron
cement
ceramics
composite
concrete
corrosion
crack
creep
ductile
elastic deformation
elastomer
fatigue
fiber
fracture
fracture toughness
galvanic corrosion
glass
hardenability
hardness
modulus of elasticity
plastic deformation
Poisson's ratio
polymer

polymer matrix composite
shear modulus
stainless steel
steel
strain
stress
stress corrosion cracking
tensile strength
thermoplastic
thermoset
tribology
wear
yield strength
Young's modulus

MECHANICS AND DYNAMICS

bending moment
buckling
center of gravity
centroid
constitutive equation
couple
critical speed
curvature
damping
distributed force
equilibrium
excitation
finite element analysis
forced vibration
free-body diagram
free vibration
impulse
inertia
isolation
kinetic energy
mechanical testing
modal analysis
mode
moment

moment of inertia
momentum
particle kinematics
particle kinetics
plane strain
plane stress
Portland cement
projectile
random vibration
rigid body
rotation
shear
shear force
shear stress

statics
stress concentration
stress relaxation
tensile stress
tension
tensor
thermal stress
thrust
torque
torsion
truss
uniaxial
vibration
viscoelastic

A–Z

Aa

---

ac|cel|er|a|tion /æksɛləreɪʃⁿn/

GENERAL

NOUN **Acceleration** is the rate at which velocity changes.

○ The vehicle has an acceleration of 0 to 60 miles per hour in 4.8 seconds.

○ The acceleration due to gravity, g, is 9.81ms-2.

---

ac|cel|er|om|e|ter /æksɛlərɒmɪtər/ (**accelerometers**)

CONTROL, INSTRUMENTATION AND METROLOGY

NOUN An **accelerometer** is a device for measuring the acceleration of a vibrating object.

○ Accelerometers measure vibrations of the machine.

○ Vibratory motion is often sensed by using an accelerometer attached to the vibrating object.

> **WORD BUILDER**
> **-meter** = measuring instrument
>
> The suffix **-meter** is often used for instruments that measure things: **interferometer**, **manometer**, **micrometer**, **thermometer**.

---

ac|tu|a|tor /æktʃueɪtər/ (**actuators**)

CONTROL, INSTRUMENTATION AND METROLOGY

NOUN An **actuator** is a machine or part of a machine which moves or controls another part in response to an input.

○ The motors in the robot arm are actuators that make the arm move.

○ Most computer-controlled actuators are electromechanical devices that convert the output commands from the computer into mechanical action.

WORD BUILDER

-or = performing

The suffix **-or** is often used to form words connected with performing a particular function: **compressor**, **governor**, **manipulator**, **regulator**, **sensor**.

---

a|dap|tive /ədæptɪv/

CONTROL, INSTRUMENTATION AND METROLOGY

ADJECTIVE Adaptive is used to describe systems that can change their parameters as the conditions change.

○ Adaptive cruise control can adjust the speed of the car in relation to the vehicle ahead.

○ An adaptive controller modifies its characteristics to deal with new situations.

▶ COLLOCATIONS:
adaptive control
adaptive system

---

ad|he|sive /ædhisɪv/

MATERIALS

NOUN Adhesive is a sticky substance used for joining two things together.

○ Use a strong adhesive to stick the mirror in place.

○ The adhesive chosen should have enough tackiness to attach the device securely to the tissue surface.

---

air-con|di|tion|ing /ɛər kəndɪʃənɪŋ/

ENERGY, THERMODYNAMICS AND HEAT TRANSFER

NOUN Air-conditioning is a system for controlling the temperature and humidity of air.

○ If it gets too hot, close the windows and turn on the air-conditioning.

○ The vehicle's air-conditioning system keeps the interior of the car cool in hot weather.

---

air-cool /ɛər kul/ (air-cools, air-cooled, air-cooling)

ENERGY, THERMODYNAMICS AND HEAT TRANSFER

VERB If an engine, process, or machine is **air-cooled**, it is made colder by a flow of air.

○ The engine is air-cooled by a flow of air from the fan.

○ Some systems use a water-cooled heat exchanger in the summer and an air-cooled one in the winter.

---

air-in|take /ɛər ınteık/ (air-intakes)

FLUID ENGINEERING

NOUN An **air-intake** is an opening through which air enters an engine or system, usually for combustion or cooling.

○ Air is drawn into the engine through the air-intake.

○ The airflow first passes through the air-intake when approaching the engine.

---

air tur|bine /ɛər tɜrbın/ (air turbines)

FLUID ENGINEERING

NOUN An **air turbine** is a small turbine driven by compressed air, especially one used as a starter for engines.

○ The compressed air is then let into air turbines to produce mechanical energy.

○ Compressed air is used to drive an air turbine which in turn drives the engine shaft with a clutch.

---

al|loy /ælɔı/ (alloys)

MATERIALS

NOUN An **alloy** is a metal which is not pure because other elements have been added to it.

○ Melting aluminum with a small amount of copper produces the alloy duralumin.

○ Like other copper alloys, Cu-Ni alloys possess excellent mechanical properties at low temperatures.

---

an|neal|ing /ənílɪŋ/

MANUFACTURING AND ASSEMBLY

NOUN **Annealing** is the process of heating a metal or alloy to a temperature below its melting point in order to make it softer.

○ The brass is then heated in a process known as annealing, softening it so that it does not split.

○ Annealing involves heating a metal to a suitable temperature and holding it there, followed by cooling it at a suitable rate to lower the hardness.

---

an|vil /ænvɪl/ (anvils)

CONTROL, INSTRUMENTATION AND METROLOGY

NOUN An **anvil** is a fixed part of a measuring device. The piece to be measured is held against it.

○ The sample rests against the micrometer's anvil and the spindle moves toward it.

○ The movable anvil is pressed against the workpiece by a light pressure and measures the size of the workpiece.

---

ar|bor /ɑrbər/ (arbors)

MANUFACTURING AND ASSEMBLY

NOUN An **arbor** is a rotating bar in a machine or power tool on which a milling cutter or grinding wheel is fitted.

○ I have a problem with my electric saw. The arbor spins but the blade won't cut.

○ The milling cutter is mounted on a part called an arbor held by an electrically operated spindle.

ar|ti|fi|cial in|tel|li|gence (ABBR **AI**) /ˌɑːtɪfɪʃ³l ɪntɛlɪdʒ³ns/

CONTROL, INSTRUMENTATION AND METROLOGY

NOUN   **Artificial intelligence** is a type of computer technology which is concerned with making machines carry out work in an intelligent way, similar to the way a human would.

○ *Artificial intelligence is about making computers act more like humans.*

○ *All artificial intelligence designs are inspired by the human brain.*

as|sem|bly /əsɛmbli/

MANUFACTURING AND ASSEMBLY

NOUN   **Assembly** is the process of putting parts together to make a machine or other product.

○ *All the components were made and ready for assembly.*

○ *The apparatus comes in kit form for ease of assembly.*

as|sem|bly line /əsɛmbli laɪn/ (**assembly lines**)

MANUFACTURING AND ASSEMBLY

NOUN   An **assembly line** is an arrangement of workers and machines in a factory, where each worker deals with only one part of a product. The product passes from one worker to another until it is finished.

○ *To speed up production, he set up an assembly line, with each worker producing a different part of the tool.*

○ *At least 200 women worked in the main factory, on assembly lines running down the length of the building.*

at|om|ize /ˈætəmaɪz/ (**atomizes, atomized, atomizing**)

FLUID ENGINEERING

VERB   If a liquid fuel is **atomized**, it is made into a fine spray so that it will burn more easily.

○ *When the fuel is atomized, it mixes with the air and ignites.*

○ *The gas must be atomized, that is broken up into small droplets and mixed with air.*

A

▶ **SYNONYM:**
nebulize

▶ **COLLOCATIONS:**
atomize fuel
atomize gas

---

at|om|iz|er /ˈætəmaɪzər/ (**atomizers**)

FLUID ENGINEERING

NOUN An **atomizer** is a device that produces a fine spray from a liquid.

○ Most combustors use an atomizer in which fuel is forced under high pressure through a hole.

○ Atomizers are used to spray paint.

▶ **SYNONYM:**
nebulizer

---

ax|le /ˈæksəl/ (**axles**)

MACHINERY AND COMPONENTS

NOUN An **axle** is a rotating bar on which a wheel, a pair of wheels, or another rotating part is attached.

○ As the car went over a bump in the road, the rear axle snapped and a wheel fell off.

○ Trucks always had two wheels on the front axle and four wheels on each of the others, with the exception of a few.

Bb

---

back|lash /bæklæʃ/

MACHINERY AND COMPONENTS

NOUN **Backlash** occurs when the slack in a system of gears causes the gears to start to turn in the opposite direction.

○ *Most backlash damage is done when gears stop rotating in one direction and start rotating in the opposite direction.*

○ *If one gear moves and the other is stationary, there is a backlash, but if both gears move simultaneously, there is no backlash.*

---

baf|fle /bæfᵊl/ (baffles)

FLUID ENGINEERING

NOUN A **baffle** is a thin flat object which is hung in a flow of liquid or gas to cause partial obstruction.

○ *The water is forced to pass under the baffles, slowing down the flow.*

○ *A number of different baffles are used to promote cross flow.*

---

ball|and|sock|et joint /bɔl ənd sɒkɪt dʒɔɪnt/ (ball-and-socket joints)

MACHINERY AND COMPONENTS

NOUN A **ball and socket joint** is a type of coupling consisting of a ball-shaped part that fits into a ball-shaped socket.

○ *The ball-and-socket joint in your car connects your steering mechanism to your wheels so you can turn the vehicle left and right.*

○ *Ball-and-socket joints are triaxial joints that allow rotation about three axes.*

B

RELATED WORDS

Compare **ball-and-socket joint** with the following words:

knuckle joint
a hinged joint between two rods

universal joint
a joint between two rotating shafts that allows them to move at
any angle and in all directions

---

ball bear|ing /bɔl bɛərɪŋ/ (ball bearings)

MACHINERY AND COMPONENTS

NOUN A **ball bearing** is a bearing containing hard steel balls.

○ Ball bearings are made of small steel balls and are used in bicycles to make the
  wheels and steering move more smoothly.

○ The steel balls act as ball bearings so that the action is smoother than just
  one gear turning against another.

---

ball valve /bɔl vælv/ (ball valves)

FLUID ENGINEERING

NOUN A **ball valve** is a valve consisting of a metal ball with a hole in it.
When the valve is open, a fluid can flow through the hole.

○ When the ball valves are open, their holes line up with the pipe and the oil can
  flow through.

○ One type of ball valve has a ball that is smaller than the passageway so there
  is significant flow restriction as the fluid passes through.

---

bay|o|net /beɪənɪt/ (bayonets)

MACHINERY AND COMPONENTS

NOUN A **bayonet** is a type of fastening in which a cylindrical part is
pushed into a socket and turned so that pins on its side fit into grooves
in the socket.

○ Many types of light bulbs are fitted with bayonet connectors.

○A bayonet adapter, consisting of a cylindrical shaped part with holding pins that threads into the thermocouple hole, is used to retain a spring loaded thermocouple.

b

beam /biːm/ (beams)

GENERAL

NOUN A **beam** is a horizontal part of a structure used to carry a load.

○Steel beams supported the roof.

○When a vertical load is applied to a horizontal beam it will bend.

bear|ing /bɛərɪŋ/ (bearings)

MACHINERY AND COMPONENTS

NOUN A **bearing** is a device that supports moving parts and allows them to move more smoothly by reducing friction.

○The wheel bearings in your car allow the wheel to turn smoothly without any friction.

○The bearings support axial loads of thousands of newtons in either direction.

bed /bɛd/ (beds)

MANUFACTURING AND ASSEMBLY

NOUN The **bed** of a machine is the base on which a moving part carrying a tool or workpiece rests.

○First, lay the wood on the bed of the machine.

○The lathe should be set up so the cutting tool feeds automatically along the bed of the lathe.

belt drive /bɛlt draɪv/ (belt drives)

MACHINERY AND COMPONENTS

NOUN A **belt drive** is a transmission system that uses a flexible strip to transfer power.

○The turning disk is connected by a belt drive to the electric motor.

○A rubber belt drive is used to transfer power from one pulley to another.

B

bend|ing mo|ment /bɛndɪŋ moʊmənt/ (**bending moments**)

MECHANICS AND DYNAMICS

NOUN A **bending moment** is a moment that makes a bar or beam bend and which may vary along the length of the bar or beam.

○ *The bending moment in a door lintel is largest at its center.*

○ *The bending moment in a horizontal beam is the moment of the vertical force or load applied to the beam that produces bending.*

bev|el gear /bɛvᵊl gɪər/ (**bevel gears**)

MACHINERY AND COMPONENTS

NOUN **Bevel gears** are cone-shaped gears whose teeth mesh together to transmit power between two shafts that are at an angle to each other.

○ *The tooth-bearing surfaces of bevel gears have a conical shape.*

○ *The shape of a bevel gear allows it to mesh with another gear whose axis is at an angle to it.*

bil|let /bɪlɪt/ (**billets**)

GENERAL

NOUN A **billet** is a length of metal that has been partly processed but is not in its final state.

○ *The semi-finished steel billets are then re-rolled or forged into other forms.*

○ *Connecting rods are sometimes machined out of a solid billet of metal.*

bit /bɪt/ (**bits**)

MANUFACTURING AND ASSEMBLY

NOUN A **bit** is a tool for cutting or drilling that is usually held by a drill.

○ *There are different sized drill bits for drilling different sized holes.*

○ *The gouge bit is sharpened on the bottom edge only because if the sides are sharp they will enlarge the hole as the drill advances.*

blank¹ /blæŋk/ (blanks)

FLUID ENGINEERING

NOUN A **blank** is a plate or a small round piece of a metal, plastic, or other material used to seal a hole.

○ All unused connectors should be sealed with blanks.

○ You can remove the sensors from your bumper, but you will have to put blanks in to cover the holes.

blank² /blæŋk/ (blanks, blanked, blanking)

MANUFACTURING AND ASSEMBLY

VERB If a piece of metal is **blanked**, it is forged, stamped, punched, or cut out so that is ready for forging, die casting, or drawing.

○ When the sheet metal has been blanked, the resulting disks are then shaped by being bent in dies.

○ The disks are blanked from sheet stock and passed immediately into a die stack.

bleed /bliːd/ (bleeds, bled, bleeding)

FLUID ENGINEERING

VERB If you **bleed** a container or an enclosed system, you remove liquid or gas from it.

○ Bleed the radiators regularly to release trapped air and make them work efficiently.

○ They need to bleed the hydraulic system to remove all the air.

bleed valve /bliːd vælv/ (bleed valves)

FLUID ENGINEERING

NOUN A **bleed valve** is a valve for removing liquid from a tank or tube, or for removing gas from a liquid.

○ The calipers of hydraulic brakes are fitted with bleed valves to allow trapped air to be removed.

○ The manual bleed valve allows the manual release of air pressure from the tire.

blow mold|ing (BRIT **blow moulding**) /bloʊ moʊldɪŋ/

MANUFACTURING AND ASSEMBLY

NOUN **Blow molding** is a process for forming plastic objects in which plastic is melted, put in a mold, and then shaped by having compressed air blown into it.

○ Blow molding is a process in which hollow plastic objects, such as drinks bottles, are formed.

○ The basic principle of blow molding is to inflate a softened thermoplastic hollow preform against the cooled surface of a closed mold, where the material solidifies into a hollow product.

boil|er /bɔɪlər/ (**boilers**)

GENERAL

NOUN A **boiler** is a container in which a liquid, usually water, is heated until it changes into a vapor.

○ A boiler generates steam from water.

○ A boiler that has a loss of feed water and is allowed to boil dry can be very dangerous.

boil|ing /bɔɪlɪŋ/

ENERGY, THERMODYNAMICS AND HEAT TRANSFER

NOUN **Boiling** is the action of heating a liquid until it becomes a vapor.

○ When water reaches boiling point it evaporates into steam.

○ Boiling of fuel in the fuel lines can happen because fuel in a vacuum boils at a lower temperature.

bolt /boʊlt/ (**bolts**)

GENERAL

NOUN A **bolt** is a pin with parallel threads and a flat end, used for fastening parts together and often secured with a nut.

○ Make sure the parts to be joined together are securely held with nuts and bolts.

○ Loosen the nut from the bolt by turning it repeatedly.

RELATED WORDS

Compare **bolt** with the following words:

eyebolt
a bolt with a top part in the form of a ring so that it can be lifted, pulled, or secured more easily

nut
a small square or hexagonal block with a threaded hole through the middle for screwing on the end of a bolt

stud
a bolt without a flat top part, that is threaded at both ends but not in the center

washer
a flat ring of metal put under the head of a bolt or nut to spread the load when the bolt or nut is tightened

---

bore /bɔr/ (bores)

MANUFACTURING AND ASSEMBLY

NOUN A **bore** is a circular hole in a material produced by drilling, turning, or drawing.

○ Drill a bore of 100mm diameter into the workpiece.

○ The eyebolt is threaded into a bore in the metal.

---

bor|ing /bɔrɪŋ/

MANUFACTURING AND ASSEMBLY

NOUN **Boring** is the process of creating a larger circular hole from a hole that has already been drilled.

○ Boring done on a lathe can produce conical or cylindrical holes.

○ Boring is the enlarging of a hole by removing material from the internal surfaces with a single-point cutter bit.

B

boss /bɒs/ (bosses)

MACHINERY AND COMPONENTS

NOUN A **boss** is a cylindrical or rounded knob that projects from the surface of a part and provides a place for another object to attach onto it.

○ *A propeller consists of a cylindrical boss with flat blades welded to it.*

○ *Some motors use a precisely machined boss on the front face to locate it on the mating part.*

brac|ing /breɪsɪŋ/

GENERAL

NOUN **Bracing** consists of devices that clamp parts of a structure together in order to strengthen or support it.

○ *Bracing consisting of a rigid steel frame prevents the structure from moving.*

○ *This type of bracing consists of rods passing through the entire length of the boiler, with heavy nuts and washers at the ends on the outside, and check nuts on the inside.*

brit|tle /brɪtəl/

MATERIALS

ADJECTIVE A **brittle** material breaks or splits easily.

○ *This steel is too brittle to make propeller blades because it might break whilst rotating.*

○ *Because the coke is so brittle, it can crack just from a heat cycle.*

buck|ling /bʌklɪŋ/

MECHANICS AND DYNAMICS

NOUN **Buckling** happens when a force presses on a slender structure and makes it collapse.

○ *Too great a load on the columns can cause buckling.*

○ *A slender strut under the action of an axial load will fail by buckling.*

b

burr /bɜr/ (burrs)

MANUFACTURING AND ASSEMBLY

NOUN A **burr** is a rough edge on a workpiece after it has been cut, drilled, etc.

○ File the edges of the steel to remove any burrs.

○ The burrs on the edges of the teeth must be cleaned up with a small triangular jewelers' file.

---

bush /bʊʃ/ (bushes)

MACHINERY AND COMPONENTS

NOUN A **bush** is a thin metal tube that fits into a hole or covers a part in order to guide the movement of a part or reduce friction.

○ In a bushed bearing, there is a bush made of brass between the shaft and the bearing.

○ Bushes are often used in wood to provide additional bearing area and to prevent crushing of the wood when bolts are tightened.

---

by|pass /baɪpæs/ (bypasses)

FLUID ENGINEERING

NOUN A **bypass** is a way of diverting a flow of fluid around a system.

○ There has to be a bypass – another way for water to flow around the system if all the valves are closed.

○ A bypass is a system of pipes and valves permitting the diversion of flow or pressure around a line valve.

Cc

CAD sys|tem /kæd sɪstəm/ (**CAD systems**) (short for **Computer Aided Design system**)

MANUFACTURING AND ASSEMBLY

NOUN A **CAD system** is a computer system for designing parts or products before they are manufactured.

○ A CAD system uses computer analysis to design car parts and other products.

○ Students use the computer and CAD system to create solid models of various machine components.

cage /keɪdʒ/ (**cages**)

MACHINERY AND COMPONENTS

NOUN A **cage** is a device that fits into a rolling bearing and keeps the right amount of space between its individual rollers or balls.

○ Without the cage, the balls would eventually move out of position, causing the bearing to fail.

○ Enclosing the balls or rollers of bearings in a cage prevents them from rubbing against each other and causing additional friction.

cal|i|per /kælɪpər/ (**calipers**)

CONTROL, INSTRUMENTATION AND METROLOGY

NOUN A **caliper** is a measuring device that holds the object to be measured between two metal jaws.

○ Place the tips of the caliper on each end of the sample, and read the measurement.

○ A caliper's jaws must be brought into contact with the part being measured.

cam /kæm/ (cams)

MACHINERY AND COMPONENTS

NOUN A **cam** is a sliding or rotating part of irregular profile that contacts another part and makes that part move in a backward and forward motion.

○ *The rotating cam pushes the follower up, so as the cam rotates the follower moves up and down.*

○ *A cam is a rotating or sliding part in a mechanical linkage that is used to change rotary motion into linear motion or vice versa.*

cam|shaft /kæmʃæft/ (camshafts)

MACHINERY AND COMPONENTS

NOUN A **camshaft** is a shaft with one or more cams attached to it, especially one that operates the valves in an internal combustion engine.

○ *As the camshaft rotates, the cams push against the followers to open the valves.*

○ *In an internal combustion engine with pistons, the camshaft is used to operate poppet valves.*

> **OTHER PARTS OF AN INTERNAL-COMBUSTION ENGINE INCLUDE:**
>
> crankcase, crankshaft, cylinder, poppet, sump, tappet, wrist pin

car|bon steel /kɑrbən stil/

MATERIALS

NOUN **Carbon steel** is an alloy consisting of iron and less that 1 percent carbon. It may or may not contain small amounts of other elements.

○ *Carbon steel with less than 0.2% carbon is easy to weld.*

○ *Both carbon steel and cast iron consist of iron with carbon added, but cast iron contains more carbon.*

C

car|riage /kǽrɪdʒ/ (**carriages**)

MACHINERY AND COMPONENTS

NOUN The **carriage** of a machine is the moving part that carries or holds another part.

○ *The carriage of a lathe supports, moves, and controls the cutting tool.*

○ *The carriage is then moved around the rotating workpiece, and the cutting tool gradually shaves material from the workpiece.*

cast|ing /kǽstɪŋ/

MANUFACTURING AND ASSEMBLY

NOUN **Casting** is a process in which a material such as metal or plastic in liquid form is poured into a mold and allowed to become hard, in order to make parts or products.

○ *Casting is the most efficient way of making complex metal shapes.*

○ *Intricately shaped components that are difficult to produce by other methods can be produced by casting.*

cast i|ron /kǽst aɪərn/

MATERIALS

NOUN **Cast iron** is an alloy consisting of iron with around 4 percent carbon. It may or may not contain small amounts of other elements.

○ *Cast iron is used for car engines because it is easily made into complex shapes.*

○ *Cast iron, with its high carbon content and low melting temperature, is ideal for the production of fittings by casting.*

ce|ment /sɪmɛnt/

MATERIALS

NOUN **Cement** is a powder consisting of a mixture of minerals that becomes hard when water is added. It is often mixed with sand and small stones to make concrete.

○ *Cement can be mixed with sand, gravel, and water to make concrete.*

○ *Concrete is a combination of cement and an aggregate.*

cen|ter (BRIT **centre**) /sɛntər/ (**centers**)

MANUFACTURING AND ASSEMBLY

NOUN A **center** is a pointed tool mounted in a lathe on which a workpiece can be turned or ground.

○ *Position the workpiece between the centers of the lathe.*

○ *Mount the workpiece on a center in the headstock.*

cen|ter of grav|i|ty (BRIT **centre of gravity**) /sɛntər əv grævɪti/ (**center of gravitys**)

MECHANICS AND DYNAMICS

NOUN The **center of gravity** of a body is the point where there is equal mass on all sides.

○ *A low center of gravity makes automobiles more stable.*

○ *The center of gravity of an airplane is the point where it would balance if it were possible to suspend it at that point.*

cen|trif|u|gal force /sɛntrɪfyəgəl fɔrs/

GENERAL

NOUN **Centrifugal force** is the tendency of an object moving in a circle to travel away from the center of the circle.

○ *Centrifugal force is what makes a propeller blade fly off if it breaks at the root.*

○ *Centrifugal force is the outward force, away from the axis of rotation, acting on a revolving object.*

cen|trif|u|gal pump /sɛntrɪfyəgəl pʌmp/ (**centrifugal pumps**)

FLUID ENGINEERING

NOUN A **centrifugal pump** is a pump that uses an impeller (=a rotating part) to move a liquid around in a circular movement.

○ *Water is circulated using a centrifugal pump.*

○ *In a centrifugal pump, the pressure is developed partly by centrifugal force and partly by the lifting action of the impellers on the water.*

C

cen|troid /sɛntrɔɪd/ (**centroids**)

MECHANICS AND DYNAMICS

NOUN The **centroid** of a body is the point where there is equal volume on all sides.

o *The centroid of a solid body made from a single material is the center of its mass.*

o *If the mass of a body is distributed evenly, then the centroid and center of mass are the same.*

ce|ram|ics /sɪræmɪks/

MATERIALS

NOUN **Ceramics** are solids formed by heating a mixture of minerals and then cooling it.

o *Ceramics are more resistant to high temperatures than are metals.*

o *Traditionally, ceramics were made from clay, but now they are made from substances such as alumina and synthetic materials.*

chain drive /tʃeɪn draɪv/ (**chain drives**)

MACHINERY AND COMPONENTS

NOUN A **chain drive** is a chain of links passing over sprockets that makes one shaft start rotating another.

o *In a motorcycle chain drive, a sprocket mounted in the engine output shaft is connected to a sprocket attached to the back wheel by a metal chain.*

o *A chain drive is a mechanism consisting of a chain or chains for transmitting power.*

chat|ter /tʃætər/ (**chatters, chattered, chattering**)

MANUFACTURING AND ASSEMBLY

VERB If a machine part **chatters** it makes contact with a workpiece in an intermittent way, often causing damage to the workpiece.

o *If stainless steel is cut at too low a speed, the tool may chatter, producing a poor surface.*

o *Note whether the drill cuts smoothly and rapidly, or whether it jumps and chatters.*

check valve /tʃɛk vælv/ (check valves)

FLUID ENGINEERING

NOUN A **check valve** is a valve that is closed by the pressure of a fluid so that the fluid does not flow back in the direction it came from.

○ *Check valves ensure that fuel flows in only one direction, thus avoiding contamination.*

○ *The special coupling device contains a check valve that allows fluid to pass downward but not upward through the casing.*

chip /tʃɪp/ (chips)

MANUFACTURING AND ASSEMBLY

NOUN **Chips** are small pieces of material that come off the surface of a workpiece when it is being cut.

○ *When cutting metal, make sure that the chips clear properly and do not scratch the surface of the metal.*

○ *Chips are pieces of metal removed from a workpiece by cutting tools or by an abrasive medium.*

choke /tʃoʊk/ (chokes)

FLUID ENGINEERING

NOUN A **choke** is a device for reducing the flow of a fluid in a pipe or tube.

○ *The choke on a motorcycle restricts the amount of air that is mixed with the gas.*

○ *A choke is a device that restricts the flow of air at the entrance of the carburetor.*

chuck /tʃʌk/ (chucks)

MANUFACTURING AND ASSEMBLY

NOUN A **chuck** is a device that holds a workpiece in a lathe or a tool in a drill. It has two jaws that move together to keep the workpiece or tool in a central position.

○ *The drill bit is held by the chuck of the drill.*

○ *The workpiece must be securely attached to the chuck when the lathe is operating.*

clutch /klʌtʃ/ (clutchs)

MACHINERY AND COMPONENTS

NOUN A **clutch** is a device that locks two parts of a mechanism together and transfers power between them.

○ Clutches control whether automobiles transmit engine power to the gearbox.

○ If the engine is running with the clutch engaged and the transmission in neutral, the engine spins the input shaft of the transmission, but no power is transmitted to the wheels.

C|M|M /si εm εm/ (short for **Coordinate Measurement Machine**)

CONTROL, INSTRUMENTATION AND METROLOGY

ABBREVIATION A **CMM** is a robot used for measuring the shape of a component by touching it repeatedly with a probe (= a long thin electronic sensing device).

○ The CMM was programmed to measure the specimen at 400 different positions, thus producing a map of its shape.

○ It takes two or three days to program the CMM and run the measurements.

> **PRONUNCIATION**
>
> Three-letter abbreviations are usually pronounced as separate letters with the stress on the last syllable.
> **CMM** /si εm εm/
> **CNC** /si εn si/
> **PID** /pi aɪ di/

C|N|C /si εn si/ (short for **Computer Numerical Control**)

MANUFACTURING AND ASSEMBLY

ABBREVIATION **CNC** is a way of controlling how machine tools operate using a computer.

○ CNC machine tools have revolutionized manufacturing because they are operated by computers, not people.

○ CNC operators who have substantial training in numerical control programming may advance to the job of tool programmer.

cog /kɒg/ (**cogs**)

MACHINERY AND COMPONENTS

NOUN A **cog** is a tooth at the edge of a gear wheel or sprocket.

○ *The cogs of the gears mesh together as they turn.*

○ *This large wheel has teeth, or cogs, in its rim.*

coil spring /kɔɪl sprɪŋ/ (**coil springs**)

MACHINERY AND COMPONENTS

NOUN A **coil spring** is a spring formed from a wire or rod twisted in a spiral shape.

○ *Coil springs are an integral part of a car's front suspension.*

○ *Constant overloading can cause coil springs to fail, so they will not compress or rebound.*

cold shut /kould ʃʌt/ (**cold shuts**)

MANUFACTURING AND ASSEMBLY

NOUN A **cold shut** is a fault in the surface of a piece of metal caused by two streams of molten metal not joining properly when the piece is being cast.

○ *Check for defects such as cracks and cold shuts in the castings.*

○ *A cold shut is a discontinuity that appears on the surface of cast metal as a result of two streams of liquid meeting and failing to unite.*

cold work|ing /kould wɜrkɪŋ/

MANUFACTURING AND ASSEMBLY

NOUN **Cold working** is a process in which metal is shaped at a fairly low temperature. This increases the metal's yield strength but makes it less ductile.

○ *The strength and hardness of steel can be increased by cold working, but that will also make it less ductile.*

○ *The 300 series of stainless steels cannot be hardened by heat treatment but can be hardened by cold working.*

C

col|lar /ˈkɒlər/ (collars)

MACHINERY AND COMPONENTS

NOUN A **collar** is a ring or tube that fits onto a shaft or rod, for example to prevent a part from coming off the end of a shaft.

o There's a metal collar around the shaft that prevents it from being pulled out.

o Threaded shaft collars lock securely by fully slotting into the threads of the shaft.

com|bus|tion /kəmˈbʌstʃən/

ENERGY, THERMODYNAMICS AND HEAT TRANSFER

NOUN **Combustion** is the process in which a fuel burns in oxygen.

o The color of the flame during combustion of a fuel can tell you if the fuel is getting enough oxygen for burning.

o Combustion is a process involving the reaction of a fuel and an oxidizer, in which the chemical energy stored in the fuel is released.

> **WORD BUILDER**
> **-ion** = process
>
> The suffix **-ion** often changes a verb into a noun, meaning the "process of doing something:" **combustion**, **insulation**, **refrigeration**, **vibration**.

com|po|site /kəmˈpɒzɪt/ (composites)

MATERIALS

NOUN A **composite** is a mixture of two materials, one of which makes the other stronger.

o The commonest composites in current use are plastics, reinforced by glass or carbon fibers.

o Fiber-reinforced plastic is a composite made of a polymer matrix reinforced with fibers.

com|pres|sion /kəmprɛʃ°n/

GENERAL

NOUN **Compression** is the action of applying a force to a solid, liquid, or gas so that it takes up less space.

○ *Scrap car bodies are crushed by compression between two large anvils.*

○ *A column will buckle under compression if it is too slender.*

com|pres|sor /kəmprɛsər/ (**compressors**)

ENERGY, THERMODYNAMICS AND HEAT TRANSFER

NOUN The **compressor** of a gas turbine is the part that compresses the air before it enters the combustion chambers.

○ *The compressor of a jet engine is a large fan which draws air into the air-intake.*

○ *Air compressors are machines that compress air to higher than atmospheric pressures for delivery to pneumatic or robotic tools or other equipment.*

com|pu|ter-aid|ed pro|cess plan|ning (ABBR **CAPP**)
/kəmpyutər eɪdɪd prɒsɛs plænɪŋ/

MANUFACTURING AND ASSEMBLY

NOUN **Computer-aided process planning** is a way of planning a complex manufacturing process using computers.

○ *Computer-aided process planning was used to establish the best possible sequence of production operations for the washing machines.*

○ *Computer-aided process planning software helps plan manufacturing processes by analyzing different routing alternatives to streamline the flow of work in a process through the plant.*

con|crete /kɒŋkrit/

MATERIALS

NOUN **Concrete** is a hard substance made by mixing cement, sand, and small stones.

○ *The floor was made of solid concrete.*

○ *Concrete is a composite construction material composed of cement, gravel, and water.*

con|den|sa|tion /kɒndɛnseɪʃᵊn/

ENERGY, THERMODYNAMICS AND HEAT TRANSFER

NOUN **Condensation** is the process in which a vapor touches a cool surface and turns into a liquid.

○ *Condensation forms on windows when water vapor makes contact with the cool glass.*

○ *Condensation of vapor on a surface takes place when the surface temperature is lower than the saturation temperature.*

con|duc|tion /kəndʌkʃᵊn/

ENERGY, THERMODYNAMICS AND HEAT TRANSFER

NOUN **Conduction** is the flow of heat through a solid.

○ *The canister walls, which are in contact with the metal cask wall, transfer this heat by conduction.*

○ *Conduction is heat transfer resulting from the energy exchange between molecules, due to molecular contact.*

> **RELATED WORDS**
>
> Compare **conduction** with **convection**, which is the flow of heat by the movement of a warmed gas.

con|nect|ing rod (ABBR **con rod**) /kənɛktɪŋ rɒd/ (**connecting rods**)

MACHINERY AND COMPONENTS

NOUN A **connecting rod** is a bar that connects a moving part to another part in order to make that part move.

○ *The reciprocating motion of the piston is converted into the rotary motion of the crankshaft by means of a connecting rod.*

○ *A connecting rod is a steel rod connecting the cross-head and the crankpin in an engine.*

con|sti|tu|tive e|qua|tion /kɒnstɪtutɪv ɪkweɪʒ³n/
(**constitutive equations**)

MECHANICS AND DYNAMICS

NOUN A **constitutive equation** is an equation that describes the relationship between two physical quantities, for example between the stress put on a material and the strain produced on it.

○ The constitutive equation for most metals is based on Hooke's law.

○ Constitutive equations, such as Hooke's law for linear elastic materials, describe the stress-strain relationship in calculations.

con|trol¹ /kəntroʊl/

CONTROL, INSTRUMENTATION AND METROLOGY

NOUN **Control** of a machine or process is designing it so that it behaves in a particular way, by continually measuring the output and changing the input in response.

○ The way in which furnace temperature is held constant by use of a thermostat is a simple example of control.

○ These valves are widely used in the automatic control of steam and other industrial fluids.

con|trol² /kəntroʊl/ (**controls**)

MACHINERY AND COMPONENTS

NOUN A **control** is a device that regulates how a machine operates.

○ The machine has a control that allows the operator to adjust it to the most efficient operating speed.

○ The battery master switch is a control that cuts power from the battery to the other components of the vehicle.

con|trol|ler bi|as /kəntroʊlər baɪəs/

CONTROL, INSTRUMENTATION AND METROLOGY

NOUN In a control loop, the **controller bias** is a constant amount added to or subtracted from the action that a controller would normally take with a particular gain.

C

○ *It was necessary to introduce a controller bias because the thermocouple was not properly placed in the furnace.*

○ *The controller bias is a constant offset applied to the controller output.*

con|trol|ler gain /kəntroʊlər geɪn/

CONTROL, INSTRUMENTATION AND METROLOGY

NOUN In a control loop, the **controller gain** is the strength of action a controller will take at a particular point below or above the setpoint.

○ *As the furnace insulation became less efficient with time, it was necessary to increase the controller gain.*

○ *The controller gain defines the strength of controller response experienced in relation to a deviation between the input and output signal.*

con|trol loop /kəntroʊl lup/ (**control loops**)

CONTROL, INSTRUMENTATION AND METROLOGY

NOUN A **control loop** is a series of control operations, including measuring an output, establishing what the output should be, and taking action to correct it.

○ *The furnace temperature control loop consists of a thermocouple, a program to compare the measured temperature with the required one, and a heater which switches on if the temperature is too low.*

○ *A good example of a control loop is the action taken when adjusting hot and cold valves to maintain the water at a desired temperature.*

con|vec|tion /kənvɛkʃ°n/

ENERGY, THERMODYNAMICS AND HEAT TRANSFER

NOUN **Convection** is the flow of heat by the movement of a warmed gas.

○ *The buildings see a 30 percent saving in energy as air circulates by natural convection to the upper floors.*

○ *Convection is the transfer of heat by motion of the heated material, such as air.*

cool|ant /ˈkuːlənt/ (coolants)

ENERGY, THERMODYNAMICS AND HEAT TRANSFER

NOUN **Coolant** is a fluid used to cool a system or to transfer heat from one part of it to another.

- ○ This tank will cure overheating problems by stopping loss of coolant through the overflow pipe.
- ○ The pump circulates coolant through the cooling system.

> **WORD BUILDER**
> **-ant** = causing
>
> The suffix **-ant** is used in words for substances that have a particular effect: **coolant**, **refrigerant**.

cor|ro|sion /kəˈrouʒən/

MATERIALS

NOUN **Corrosion** is the process in which a metal is gradually destroyed by an electrochemical process.

- ○ Rust or ferric oxide is a product of corrosion.
- ○ When metals are exposed to certain environments, they detach from the surface as ions and may form compounds, such as rust. This process is called corrosion.

> **OTHER PROBLEMS THAT MAY OCCUR WITH METALS INCLUDE:**
>
> cold shuts, cracks, fractures, galvanic corrosion, stress corrosion cracking

cou|ple /ˈkʌpəl/ (couples)

MECHANICS AND DYNAMICS

NOUN A **couple** consists of two parallel forces acting at different points on a body, often making it rotate.

- ○ The jaws of a spanner introduce a couple acting on the nut to rotate it.

○ *If two equal and opposite forces act so that their lines of action are a distance apart, the result is a pure turning effort known as a couple.*

---

cou|pler /kʌplər/ (couplers)

MACHINERY AND COMPONENTS

NOUN A **coupler** is a link or rod that moves power between two rotating parts.

○ *The motor shaft is connected to the gear shaft using a flexible coupler.*

○ *There is a direct coupler between the rotating throttle shaft and the motor – there are no cams, arms etc.*

---

cou|pling /kʌplɪŋ/ (couplings)

MACHINERY AND COMPONENTS

NOUN A **coupling** is a device that connects two things together.

○ *A coupling came loose causing the trailer to break away from the vehicle.*

○ *The gear couplings that we produce are used to join the various motors and gearboxes so that the motors work efficiently.*

---

crack /kræk/ (cracks)

MATERIALS

NOUN A **crack** is a long thin hole with sharp ends in a material.

○ *The failure started from a crack in one of the welds.*

○ *To repair a crack in the tank you first need to know what caused it to crack.*

---

crank /kræŋk/ (cranks)

MACHINERY AND COMPONENTS

NOUN A **crank** is a device for transferring motion from one part to another or for changing one type of motion to another. It consists of an arm sticking out from a shaft.

○ *The drum is connected to the crank by a train of wheels, so that as the crank rotates the drum also turns.*

○*A crank is an arm attached at right angles to a rotating shaft by which reciprocating motion is given to or received from the shaft.*

---

crank|case /kræŋkkeɪs/ (**crankcases**)

MACHINERY AND COMPONENTS

NOUN The **crankcase** is the metal housing around the crankshaft, connecting rods, etc., in something such as an internal-combustion engine or a reciprocating pump.

○*The two halves of the crankcase must be separated to service the crankshaft.*

○*The housing for the crankshaft is called the crankcase.*

---

crank|shaft /kræŋkʃæft/ (**crankshafts**)

MACHINERY AND COMPONENTS

NOUN A **crankshaft** is a shaft with one or more cranks, especially the main shaft of an internal-combustion engine to which the connecting rods are attached.

○*The crankshaft in high-performance car engines needs to be carefully balanced so that it does not cause excessive vibrations.*

○*The connecting rod rocks to and fro as the crankshaft rotates.*

---

creep /kriːp/

MATERIALS

NOUN **Creep** is the tendency of a solid material to move or change shape slightly as a result of stress that continues for some time.

○*As the stress continues, the extension of the metal caused by creep eventually leads to failure.*

○*During creep, damage accumulates in the form of internal cavities.*

---

crit|i|cal speed /krɪtɪkəl spiːd/ (**critical speeds**)

MECHANICS AND DYNAMICS

NOUN The **critical speed** of a body is the speed, usually the speed at which it is rotating, at which it starts to vibrate.

C

- ○ Excessive levels of vibration while passing through a critical speed can lead to severe damage to equipment.
- ○ When the airflow over the tip of the blade reaches its critical speed, drag and torque resistance increase rapidly and shock waves form creating a sharp increase in noise.

---

cross|head /krɔshɛd/ (crossheads)

MACHINERY AND COMPONENTS

NOUN A **crosshead** is a block or bar between the piston and the connecting rod of an engine, that prevents the piston from moving from side to side and damaging the piston and cylinder.

- ○ The crosshead guides the piston rod, protecting it from the sideways forces of the connecting rod.
- ○ The hinge between the piston and connecting rod is placed outside the cylinder, in a large sliding bearing block called a crosshead.

---

cross-sec|tion /krɔs sɛkʃ°n/ (cross-sections)

GENERAL

NOUN A **cross-section** of an object is what you would see if you slice through it.

- ○ Figure 5 is a cross-section of the engine showing its internal components.
- ○ Imagine cutting the cylinder in half so you could see it in cross-section.

---

cruise con|trol /kruz kəntroʊl/

CONTROL, INSTRUMENTATION AND METROLOGY

NOUN **Cruise control** is a type of control used in vehicles to keep them moving at a particular speed.

- ○ On an empty road, the driver can set the cruise control at whatever speed he or she wants.
- ○ Cruise control is a control system that allows a vehicle to maintain a preset speed, though the driver's foot is off the accelerator.

cur|va|ture /kɜrvətʃər/

MECHANICS AND DYNAMICS

NOUN The **curvature** of a line or surface is the degree to which it is curved at a particular point.

○ *The curvature of the mirror should be gradually reduced towards its edges.*

○ *A three-dimensional surface which locally resembles that of the surface of a sphere is said to have positive curvature.*

cush|ion /kʊʃ³n/ (**cushions, cushioned, cushioning**)

MANUFACTURING AND ASSEMBLY

VERB Something that **cushions** a part or object when it hits something protects it by reducing the force of the impact.

○ *The main function of springs is to cushion the impact of a load.*

○ *The engine is cushioned against shock and vibration by rubber mountings.*

cut-off /kʌt ɔf/ (**cut-offs**)

FLUID ENGINEERING

NOUN A **cut-off** is a device that stops the flow of a fluid in a pipe or duct.

○ *This filter has an automatic cut-off mechanism to prevent the flow of water when its filtration capacity is reached.*

○ *Many cars have a fuel cut-off feature that stops the flow of fuel in the event of a collision.*

cut|ting tool /kʌtɪŋ tul/ (**cutting tools**)

MANUFACTURING AND ASSEMBLY

NOUN A **cutting tool** is a pointed tool mounted in a machine tool and used for cutting materials.

○ *Lathes and milling machines use different types of cutting tools.*

○ *Diamonds are sometimes used in cutting tools because its hardness allows it to cut other hard materials.*

cy|cle /saɪkªl/ (**cycles**)

ENERGY, THERMODYNAMICS AND HEAT TRANSFER

NOUN A **cycle** is a series of thermodynamic changes that happen to fluid, gas, or steam in an engine in order to produce power.

○ *Most internal combustion engines operate on the Otto cycle.*

○ *The phases of the cycle of a heat pump can be shown on a thermodynamic diagram.*

cyl|in|der /sɪlɪndər/ (**cylinders**)

MACHINERY AND COMPONENTS

NOUN A **cylinder** is a cavity of circular cross-section that contains a moving piston, for example in an internal combustion engine.

○ *The piston moves up in the cylinder, compressing the fuel as it goes.*

○ *Fluid may be leaking out of the back side of the master cylinder where the piston assembly goes.*

Dd

damp|ing /ˈdæmpɪŋ/

MECHANICS AND DYNAMICS

NOUN **Damping** is a reduction in vibration over a period of time.

○ Damping will eventually bring a vibrating object to rest.

○ A damping mechanism suppresses vibrations of the structure.

dash|pot /ˈdæʃpɒt/ (dashpots)

MACHINERY AND COMPONENTS

NOUN A **dashpot** is a device for reducing vibrations in which the vibrating part is attached to a piston moving in a liquid-filled cylinder.

○ A dashpot is used to dampen the effects of vibrations.

○ This type of clutch has a hydraulic dashpot to which liquid is fed to cushion the final phase of clutch engagement.

dead cen|ter (BRIT dead centre) /ˈdɛd ˈsɛntər/

MACHINERY AND COMPONENTS

NOUN **Dead center** is the exact top (**top dead center**) or bottom (**bottom dead center**) of the piston stroke in a reciprocating engine or pump.

○ The cycle begins at top dead center, when the piston is furthest away from the crankshaft.

○ A piston is at bottom dead center when it is at its lowest point.

D

die /daɪ/ (**dies**)

MANUFACTURING AND ASSEMBLY

NOUN A **die** is a shaped hollow piece into which or through which you force a material in order to produce an object of a particular shape.

○ *A metal rod is forced through a die in order to make the correct shape for the frame.*

○ *The metal is placed in a die resembling a mold.*

die cast|ing /daɪ kæstɪŋ/

MANUFACTURING AND ASSEMBLY

NOUN **Die casting** is a process in which objects of a particular shape are produced by forcing a molten material into a mold under pressure.

○ *Aluminum alloy cylinder heads are made by high-pressure die casting.*

○ *Die casting is a metal casting process in which molten metal is forced under high pressure into a mold cavity.*

RELATED WORDS

Compare **die casting** with the following words:

investment casting
a process in which a mold is made around a wax pattern. The mold is burned away when the molten material is poured in.

sand casting
a process in which molten material is poured into a mold made of sand.

---

dif|fer|en|tial¹ /dɪfərɛnʃ³l/

CONTROL, INSTRUMENTATION AND METROLOGY

ADJECTIVE **Differential** control is where the strength of the output is adjusted according to the rate of approach to the setpoint.

○ *The thermostat uses differential control which adjusts the rate of heating as the temperature approaches the setpoint.*

○ *The differential controller requires that the temperature exceed setpoint by a certain amount before the output will turn off or on again.*

dif|fer|en|tial² /dɪfərɛnʃºl/ (differentials)

MACHINERY AND COMPONENTS

NOUN A **differential** is a type of gear train (= a series of gears on a frame) that allows two shafts to rotate at different speeds while being driven by a third shaft.

○ The differential allows the car's wheels to turn at different speeds.

○ If a car did not have a differential, the wheels would have to be locked together, and would be forced to spin at the same speed.

dif|fu|sion /dɪfyuʒºn/

ENERGY, THERMODYNAMICS AND HEAT TRANSFER

NOUN **Diffusion** is the movement of atoms in a material from areas of high to low concentration.

○ Heat can increase the diffusion of carbon into the workpiece surface.

○ Atoms move from areas of high to low concentration by diffusion.

disk (BRIT disc) /dɪsk/ (disks)

GENERAL

NOUN A **disk** is a thin, flat, circular object.

○ The valve can be a circular disk or a ball.

○ A wheel is a disk-shaped object, which transfers linear motion into rotary motion and vice versa.

dis|place|ment /dɪspleɪsmənt/

MACHINERY AND COMPONENTS

NOUN **Displacement** is the volume of fluid forced out of a reciprocating pump or engine by the piston.

○ Cars with engine displacements of less than 1000cc are adequate for most domestic purposes.

○ The displacement of an engine can be increased by lengthening the crankshaft so that the piston stroke is increased.

dis|play /dɪspleɪ/ (displays)

CONTROL, INSTRUMENTATION AND METROLOGY

NOUN The **display** of a machine is the part that shows information from its sensors.

○ The reading on the display indicated that the level of carbon monoxide was rising.

○ A digital display shows the current gear, direction of travel, and many other types of vehicle information.

dis|trib|ut|ed force /dɪstrɪbyʊtɪd fɔrs/ (distributed forces)

MECHANICS AND DYNAMICS

NOUN A **distributed force** is a force that acts on a large part of a surface, not just on one place.

○ The loading on the beam can be a distributed force or a force that acts at a single point.

○ The intensity of a distributed force is the force per unit length, area, or volume.

drag /dræg/

FLUID ENGINEERING

NOUN **Drag** is the force that a fluid exerts on an object caused by a difference in velocity between the fluid and the object.

○ Drag is the force that pushes against an airplane and slows it down.

○ Drag is caused by the velocity difference between the gas and solid phases.

draw /drɔ/ (draws, drew, drawn, drawing)

MANUFACTURING AND ASSEMBLY

VERB If you **draw** a substance, you shape it by rolling it, pulling it through a die, or stretching it.

○ The metal sheet is pushed into a die in order to draw the metal into the desired shape.

○ Horizontal rollers draw molten glass from a source and flatten it into a sheet.

drill|ing /drɪlɪŋ/

MANUFACTURING AND ASSEMBLY

NOUN **Drilling** is the process of cutting holes in a solid material using a rotating cutting tool.

○ The indentation is a starting point for the drilling of the hole.

○ Drilling is a cutting process in which a drill bit is used to cut or enlarge a hole in a solid material.

drum /drʌm/ (**drums**)

MACHINERY AND COMPONENTS

NOUN A **drum** is a hollow rotating part in a steam turbine or an axial compressor (= a compressor in which gas flows parallel with the rotation of the axis).

○ The blades in a steam turbine are fastened to a cylindrical drum.

○ A rotary filter consists of a cylindrical drum covered with a perforated sieve which supports a filter cloth.

duct /dʌkt/ (**ducts**)

FLUID ENGINEERING

NOUN A **duct** is a pipe used to carry fluids at low pressures.

○ Air passing through a duct suffers a pressure drop due to friction.

○ Air enters through a duct in the front of the dryer.

duc|tile /dʌktaɪl/

MATERIALS

ADJECTIVE A **ductile** material can be easily bent, pulled, or pressed into different shapes.

○ Silver is the most ductile of metals and can be easily drawn into thin wire.

○ Ductile metals such as copper, silver, and gold have a rather large plastic deformation range.

D

> **RELATED WORDS**
>
> Compare **ductile** with **brittle**, which means "breaks or splits easily."

---

dy|nam|ic re|sponse /daɪnæmɪk rɪspɒns/

CONTROL, INSTRUMENTATION AND METROLOGY

NOUN The **dynamic response** of a machine, structure, or process is how it reacts over time to something that is done to it.

○ They investigated the dynamic response of the beam to a moving load with constant velocity.

○ The dynamic response of four types of stainless steel sheet was investigated at different strain rates.

---

dy|nam|ics /daɪnæmɪks/

GENERAL

NOUN **Dynamics** is the study of how moving objects behave.

○ Dynamics is the part of mechanics that studies movement and its causes.

○ The study of the causes of motion and changes in motion is known as dynamics.

> **RELATED WORDS**
>
> Compare **dynamics** with **statics**, which deals with objects when they are not moving.

Ee

ec|cen|tri|ci|ty or **excentricity** /ɛksɛntrɪsɪti/

MANUFACTURING AND ASSEMBLY

NOUN **Eccentricity** is how far the geometric center (= the center of a rotating part and its assembly) moves from the true center (= the center the assembly tries to rotate around naturally).

○ *Eccentricity caused the rotating shaft to rub against the sleeve.*

○ *Eccentricity is the degree to which two forms fail to share a common center.*

e|con|o|miz|er /ɪkɒnəmaɪzər/ (**economizers**)

ENERGY, THERMODYNAMICS AND HEAT TRANSFER

NOUN The **economizer** of a boiler is the part where heat is taken out of flue gas.

○ *The economizer is located between the firebox and the stack, and the hot flue gases pass through it as they move out of the firebox and into the stack.*

○ *Boiler exhaust gases pass across the economizers which are located in the exhaust ductwork and the heat is transferred to the feed water.*

ef|fi|cien|cy /ɪfɪʃ°nsi/

ENERGY, THERMODYNAMICS AND HEAT TRANSFER

NOUN The **efficiency** of a process is how near it is to being perfect.

○ *In order for cooling towers to operate at maximum efficiency, it's important to remove contaminants.*

○ *We supply high quality pistons to improve the efficiency of automobiles.*

E

e|las|tic de|for|ma|tion /ɪlæstɪk dɪfɔrmeɪʃᵊn/

MATERIALS

NOUN In **elastic deformation** a material changes shape when a stress is applied to it but goes back to its original state when the stress is removed.

○ Unlike the case of elastic deformation, these changes of shape in the material are irreversible.

○ An object in the plastic deformation range will first have undergone elastic deformation, which is reversible, so the object will return part way to its original shape.

e|las|to|mer /ɪlæstəmər/ (**elastomers**)

MATERIALS

NOUN An **elastomer** is a type of polymer that can stand very large amounts of elastic deformation.

○ Silicone is an elastomer, which has characteristics similar to rubber.

○ Rubber is an elastomer, a large molecule that can be stretched and returned to its original shape.

end ef|fec|tor /ɛnd ɪfɛktər/ (**end effectors**)

CONTROL, INSTRUMENTATION AND METROLOGY

NOUN The **end effector** of an actuator is the part that comes into contact with the object being moved or controlled.

○ The robot hand is an end effector that enables the robot to perform specified tasks.

○ In robotics, an end effector is the device at the end of a robotic arm, designed to handle objects.

en|er|gy /ɛnərdʒi/

ENERGY, THERMODYNAMICS AND HEAT TRANSFER

NOUN **Energy** is a quantity that describes how much work an object or system can do or how much heat it can produce.

○A ball flying through the air has energy because it can do "work" on an object on the ground if it collides with it, by pushing it or damaging it.

○The water is heated by solar energy.

---

en|gine /ɛndʒɪn/ (engines)

MACHINERY AND COMPONENTS

NOUN An **engine** is a machine designed to use energy, especially heat energy, to make a vehicle move.

○The purpose of a car engine is to provide the power to make the car move.

○Turn on the ignition so the car's engine is running.

---

e|qua|tion of state /ɪkweɪʒ³n əv steɪt/ (equations of state)

ENERGY, THERMODYNAMICS AND HEAT TRANSFER

NOUN The **equation of state** is the relationship between pressure, volume, and temperature for a substance.

○Solving equations of state allows us to find the volume of a gaseous mixture of chemicals at a specified temperature and pressure.

○A perfect gas obeys the simplest thermal equation of state between the pressure, the density, and the absolute temperature, using the universal gas constant.

---

e|qui|lib|ri|um[1] /ɪkwɪlɪbriəm/

ENERGY, THERMODYNAMICS AND HEAT TRANSFER

NOUN **Equilibrium** is a state in which everything stays the same.

○According to Newton's Second Law, an object that is in equilibrium will not change its speed.

○Whatever the concentrations of all the substances are at equilibrium, they remain the same forever unless a disturbance happens.

---

e|qui|lib|ri|um[2] /ɪkwɪlɪbriəm/

MECHANICS AND DYNAMICS

NOUN **Equilibrium** is the state in which all the forces on a body are exactly in balance so that the body does not move.

○ When all the forces that act on an object are balanced, then the object is said to be in a state of equilibrium.

○ An object at rest is in a state of equilibrium.

er|ror /ɛrər/ (errors)

CONTROL, INSTRUMENTATION AND METROLOGY

NOUN In a control loop, the **error** is the difference between the current value of a variable and its setpoint.

○ E is the error, the difference between the desired value (setpoint) and the latest process variable value.

○ If the temperature drops below the setpoint, the controller applies a control action to the temperature deviation (the error) and produces a control signal to increase the opening of the valve.

ex|ci|ta|tion /ɛksɪteɪʃᵊn/

MECHANICS AND DYNAMICS

NOUN **Excitation** is the act of making something vibrate.

○ If the ship's vibration is caused by the propeller, the excitation may be reduced by changing the propeller.

○ The simplest form of excitation is to pluck a stretched wire by hand so that it vibrates.

ex|haust /ɪgzɔst/

MACHINERY AND COMPONENTS

NOUN The **exhaust** of an engine consists of the waste gas that leaves it.

○ Notice the exhaust fumes coming from the back of the car.

○ The four-stroke engine uses the piston's motion to draw in fuel and air and to force out the exhaust gasses.

> **WORD BUILDER**
> **ex-** = out of
>
> The prefix **ex-** often appears in words that refer to something coming out of something: **exhaust**, **extrusion**.

ex|pan|sion /ɪkspænʃ°n/

ENERGY, THERMODYNAMICS AND HEAT TRANSFER

NOUN **Expansion** is the part of an engine cycle in which the fluid increases in volume and makes a part such as a piston or flywheel move.

○ The expansion of the gas pushes the piston inside the cylinder.

○ The expansion of the gas causes the piston to move.

e

ex|tru|sion /ɪkstruʒ°n/ (**extrusions**)

MANUFACTURING AND ASSEMBLY

NOUN An **extrusion** is a part or length of material formed by pushing a material through a die with a particular cross-section.

○ The window frames are extrusions because they are made by forcing aluminum in a plastic state through a shaped die and then cooling it.

○ Extrusions are products formed by pushing heated metal through an opening called a die, the outline of which defines the cross-sectional shape of the product.

eye|bolt /aɪboʊlt/ (**eyebolts**)

MACHINERY AND COMPONENTS

NOUN An **eyebolt** is a bolt with a top part in the form of a ring so that it can be lifted, pulled, or secured more easily.

○ Fix an eyebolt into the post; then pass a rope through the top of it.

○ An eyebolt is a ring stiffened in its lower half by the addition of a threaded shank.

Ff

face|plate /ˈfeɪspleɪt/ (faceplates)

MANUFACTURING AND ASSEMBLY

NOUN A **faceplate** is a circular metal plate used for holding workpieces in a lathe.

- When the workpiece is clamped to the faceplate of the lathe, turning can begin.
- A workpiece may be bolted or screwed to a faceplate, a large, flat disk that mounts to the spindle.

fan /fæn/ (fans)

FLUID ENGINEERING

NOUN A **fan** is a device with spinning blades that create a flow of gas.

- The fan cools the engine by blowing air over the cylinders.
- A 12V fan blows air through one end of the channel to cool the inverter and the tubes.

fa|tigue¹ /fəˈtiːg/

MATERIALS

NOUN If a material is subject to **fatigue**, it gradually cracks as stresses, especially vibrations, are repeatedly applied to it.

- There have been problems with cracking, possibly due to metal fatigue.
- A part undergoing fatigue can eventually completely fracture into two parts.

fa|tigue² /fətiɡ/ (fatigues, fatigued, fatiguing)

MATERIALS

VERB If something **fatigues** a material or part, it cracks or breaks it by repeatedly putting stresses on it, or if a material or part **fatigues** it gradually cracks or breaks.

○ *The bike's vibration fatigued the metal and eventually broke the frame.*

○ *Each revolution flexes the blade to near the elastic limit of the steel, which causes the metal to fatigue and break quickly.*

feed /fiːd/ (feeds, fed, feeding)

ENERGY, THERMODYNAMICS AND HEAT TRANSFER

VERB If a machine or furnace is **fed** with materials or fuel, or if the materials or fuel **feed** into the machine or furnace, the materials or fuel flow or move forwards into it.

○ *The machinist monitors the rate at which metal is fed into the machine for cutting.*

○ *Fuel feeds into the furnace quietly, steadily, and without smoke or dust.*

▶ SYNONYM:
supply

feed|back /fiːdbæk/

CONTROL, INSTRUMENTATION AND METROLOGY

NOUN **Feedback** is a type of control in which the error is considered when deciding future control actions.

○ *Feedback from measuring the car's speed has allowed the controller to compensate for changes to the car's speed.*

○ *The feedback component of the control checks these predictions against real time data to make appropriate corrections.*

feed|er /fiːdər/ (feeders)

MANUFACTURING AND ASSEMBLY

NOUN A **feeder** is a person or device that feeds a material into a system or machine.

○ *Film cameras use more energy than digital ones because they need a film feeder.*

○ *As each part is machined, the cutting tool creates a final cut to separate the part from the bar stock, and the feeder continues to feed the bar for the next part.*

---

fi|ber (BRIT fibre) /faɪbər/ (fibers)

MATERIALS

NOUN **Fibers** are long, thin, cylindrical parts used to strengthen polymer composites.

○ *Fiberglass is a plastic reinforced with thin glass fibers.*

○ *Carbon fibers are long, and can be carefully arranged in the resin to correspond to the main stresses to which the composite must respond.*

---

fin /fɪn/ (fins)

ENERGY, THERMODYNAMICS AND HEAT TRANSFER

NOUN A **fin** is a plate or other object which is attached to a surface in order to improve the flow of heat.

○ *The tubes may be fitted with fins to increase the heat transfer surface.*

○ *The use of fins is recognized as an effective method of increasing the heat transfer from a surface.*

---

fin|ger /fɪŋgər/ (fingers)

MACHINERY AND COMPONENTS

NOUN A **finger** is a long thin part that sticks out from a machine, especially a part that guides or protects a workpiece.

○ *Where you place the first guide finger will affect the width of your workpiece.*

○ *The locating device has a projecting finger that contacts the workpiece and is used for positioning the work-table in relation to the grinding wheel.*

---

fi|nite el|e|ment a|nal|y|sis /faɪnaɪt ɛlɪmənt ənælɪsɪs/

MECHANICS AND DYNAMICS

NOUN **Finite element analysis** is a type of computer-based analysis which calculates variations of quantities such as temperature or stress in a body by dividing it into small parts with no spaces between them.

○ *Finite element analysis is based on the idea that a solution to any complex engineering problem can be reached by subdividing the problem into smaller, more manageable elements.*

○ *Finite element analysis takes a complex problem and breaks it down into a finite number of simple problems.*

fish|plate /ˈfɪʃpleɪt/ (fishplates)

MACHINERY AND COMPONENTS

NOUN A **fishplate** is a flat piece of metal joining one rail or beam to another.

○ *The beam joints can be strengthened by iron fishplates.*

○ *A fishplate is a metal or wooden plate that is bolted to the sides of the ends of two rails or beams, to join them.*

fis|sion /ˈfɪʃ°n/

ENERGY, THERMODYNAMICS AND HEAT TRANSFER

NOUN **Fission** is a nuclear reaction in which energy is produced when atoms split apart.

○ *In nuclear fission the nucleus of an atom splits into smaller parts.*

○ *Enriched uranium gives off energy through nuclear fission.*

fit|ting /ˈfɪtɪŋ/ (fittings)

MACHINERY AND COMPONENTS

NOUN A **fitting** is a part, especially one of a standard size or shape, that goes with a larger system.

○ *They sell pipes and all types of fittings including connectors and valves.*

○ *A coupling is a fitting that is used to join two or more components together.*

fix|ture /ˈfɪkstʃər/ (fixtures)

MANUFACTURING AND ASSEMBLY

NOUN A **fixture** is a device for holding and supporting a workpiece in a machine tool.

○ Fixtures must correctly locate a workpiece with respect to a cutting tool or measuring device.

○ Fixtures are special work holding devices that are specifically designed to hold a particular workpiece.

---

flange /flænd3/ (flanges)

MACHINERY AND COMPONENTS

NOUN A **flange** is a part or edge that sticks out from an object in order to keep the object in position, strengthen it, or attach it to another object.

○ Train wheels have flanges so they do not run off the rails.

○ A flange is a projecting flat rim or collar used as an attachment.

---

flash /flæʃ/

MANUFACTURING AND ASSEMBLY

NOUN **Flash** consists of unwanted material pushed out from the edges of a die during forming.

○ A small amount of metal flows out of the die, forming flash.

○ Excess metal is squeezed out of the die cavities, forming what is referred to as flash.

---

flex|i|ble as|sem|bly sys|tem /flɛksɪbᵊl əsɛmbli sɪstəm/ (flexible assembly systems)

MANUFACTURING AND ASSEMBLY

NOUN A **flexible assembly system** is a set of machines or robots that can assemble many different kinds of products.

○ A flexible assembly system can produce a range of different products, so it meets increasing market demands for product variety.

○ The design of a flexible assembly system has the objective of reducing the rigidity that is typical of common automated systems.

---

float|ing /floʊtɪŋ/

MACHINERY AND COMPONENTS

ADJECTIVE A **floating** part or workpiece operates smoothly without touching other parts.

○ *Floating grippers have minimum contact with the workpiece and are therefore ideal for handling very sensitive workpieces.*

○ *In a floating axle, the axle shafts do not support any weight.*

---

flu|id /fluɪd/ (**fluids**)

FLUID ENGINEERING

NOUN A **fluid** is a liquid or gas.

○ *Heat can be carried by the flow of a fluid such as air or water.*

○ *A fluid is a type of matter that flows.*

---

flute /fluːt/ (**flutes**)

MANUFACTURING AND ASSEMBLY

NOUN **Flutes** are lines cut in a spiral into the surface of something, especially in a drill bit.

○ *The flutes in a drill bit help to carry the cuttings away.*

○ *The smallest microdrills do not have helical flutes like conventional drills and this makes chip removal from the hole more difficult.*

---

flux /flʌks/

ENERGY, THERMODYNAMICS AND HEAT TRANSFER

NOUN **Flux** is a movement of mass or heat caused by a change of concentration or temperature.

○ *Most of the heat flux in welding is from the weld into the workpiece.*

○ *Heat flux sensors are used to measure the rate of heat flow in many applications.*

---

fly|wheel /flaɪwiːl/ (**flywheels**)

MACHINERY AND COMPONENTS

NOUN A **flywheel** is a heavy wheel that makes an engine move smoothly by storing kinetic energy and keeping the engine at a constant speed throughout its cycle.

○ *Without a flywheel, car engines would be very jerky.*

○ *The flywheel stores energy and makes the pistons move at a constant speed.*

F

fol|low|er /fɒloʊər/ (followers)

MACHINERY AND COMPONENTS

NOUN A **follower** is a machine part that moves by being pushed or pulled by another part.

○ The follower is level for most of the cam's rotation, then is suddenly pushed up at regular intervals to open the valves.

○ A cam changes the input motion, which is usually rotary motion, to a reciprocating motion of the follower.

force /fɔrs/ (forces)

GENERAL

NOUN A **force** is an action applied to a body which makes it change speed, direction, or shape.

○ Acceleration is produced when a force acts on a body which does not resist it. Otherwise, the force will deform the body.

○ When a force is applied to an unresisting object, the object moves.

forced con|vec|tion /fɔrst kənvɛkʃⁿn/

ENERGY, THERMODYNAMICS AND HEAT TRANSFER

NOUN **Forced convection** is convection in which the movement of fluid does not happen naturally but is helped by a device such as a fan or pump.

○ With forced convection, you control the movement of the warm or cool fluid.

○ If air is blown on a hot plate by a blower, heat transfer occurs by forced convection.

forced vi|bra|tion /fɔrst vaɪbreɪʃən/

MECHANICS AND DYNAMICS

NOUN **Forced vibration** is a type of vibration in which a force is repeatedly applied to a mechanical system.

○ The vibration of moving vehicle is forced vibration, because the vehicle's engine, springs, the road, etc., continue to make it vibrate.

○ Forced vibration is when an alternating force or motion is applied to a
  mechanical system, for example when a washing machine shakes due to
  an imbalance.

RELATED WORDS

Compare **forced vibration** with these words:

free vibration
a type of vibration in which a force is applied once and the
structure or part is allowed to vibrate at its natural frequency

random vibration
a type of forced vibration in which the motion follows no regular
pattern

---

forg|ing /ˈfɔːdʒɪŋ/

MANUFACTURING AND ASSEMBLY

NOUN Forging is the process of shaping metal into its finished shape by
pressing or hitting it against an anvil or die.

○ Forging used to be done with a hammer and anvil but now it is done with
  power-driven presses or hammers.

○ Forging refers to a set of metalworking processes in which metal is formed
  into different shapes using compressive forces.

---

form|ing /ˈfɔːmɪŋ/

MANUFACTURING AND ASSEMBLY

NOUN Forming is a process in which the shape of a partly finished
product, for example sheet metal, is changed using plastic
deformation.

○ During forming, force is applied to a piece of sheet metal to change its shape
  rather than remove any material.

○ Metal forming consists of a group of manufacturing methods by which the
  shape of a workpiece is changed to another shape without changing the mass
  or composition of the workpiece.

frac|ture /fræktʃər/

MATERIALS

NOUN **Fracture** is the failure of a component or structure when a crack becomes larger.

○ *Flaws in the metal can cause cracks which eventually lead to fracture.*

○ *Taken to extreme, plastic deformation ends with the fracture of the material.*

frac|ture tough|ness /fræktʃər tʌfnɪs/

MATERIALS

NOUN The **fracture toughness** of a material is how likely it is to resist fracture.

○ *Steel has a greater fracture toughness than glass.*

○ *Because of the material's low fracture toughness, once a crack forms at an imperfection it quickly leads to failure with little additional loading.*

free-bod|y di|a|gram /friː bɒdi daɪəgræm/ (**free-body diagrams**)

MECHANICS AND DYNAMICS

NOUN A **free-body diagram** is a diagram of a structure in which all supports are replaced by forces.

○ *To help analyze the bicycle frame, the engineer drew a free-body diagram in which the wheels and the points of contact of the rider were replaced by forces.*

○ *To make a free-body diagram, you isolate the body in question from all other objects then indicate the forces that are acting on it by arrows pointing in the direction of these forces.*

free vi|bra|tion /friː vaɪbreɪʃən/

MECHANICS AND DYNAMICS

NOUN **Free vibration** is a type of vibration in which a force is applied once and the structure or part is allowed to vibrate at its natural frequency.

○ *A plucked guitar string is an example of free vibration.*

○ *Free vibration occurs when a mechanical system is set off with an initial input and then allowed to vibrate freely.*

---

freez|ing /frízɪŋ/

ENERGY, THERMODYNAMICS AND HEAT TRANSFER

NOUN **Freezing** is the process in which something changes from liquid to solid as the temperature becomes lower.

○ *Freezing of water occurs at 0 degrees C.*

○ *Freezing of the water system in cold weather is a problem in steam engines.*

---

fric|tion /frɪkʃən/

GENERAL

NOUN **Friction** is the force that stops two bodies or substances that are touching from moving against each other smoothly.

○ *Friction between two metal parts can be reduced by using oil.*

○ *Friction is created by the pads rubbing against the rotor.*

RELATED WORDS

Compare **friction** with **wear**, which is the process in which material is gradually removed from one or more surfaces in contact, and **lubrication**, which is the process whereby a substance is added between surfaces that are moving against each other in order to reduce friction and wear.

---

fric|tion clutch /frɪkʃən klʌtʃ/ (**friction clutches**)

MACHINERY AND COMPONENTS

NOUN A **friction clutch** is a clutch in which the drive is transmitted by the friction between surfaces attached to the driving and driven shafts. These surfaces are lined with cork, asbestos, or other fibrous material.

○ *Cars with friction clutches need to have the linings replaced periodically.*

○ *Friction clutches are by far the most well-known type of clutches.*

fuel /fyuəl/ (fuels)

ENERGY, THERMODYNAMICS AND HEAT TRANSFER

NOUN A **fuel** is a material used to generate energy when it is burned.

○ *The coal, wood, or other fuel in a steam engine burns to create steam.*
○ *Ignition occurs as fuel is injected into the compressed and heated air.*

ful|crum /fʊlkrəm/ (fulcrums)

GENERAL

NOUN A **fulcrum** is the pivot around which a lever turns.

○ *The brake lever stopped working because it had become detached from the fulcrum.*
○ *They moved the boulder using a stone as the fulcrum and a crowbar as the lever.*

fur|nace /fɜrnɪs/ (furnaces)

GENERAL

NOUN A **furnace** is an enclosed chamber in which heat is produced, for example to generate steam, burn waste, or produce molten metal.

○ *The aluminum is melted in a furnace at a temperature of 1400 degrees.*
○ *The iron ore is melted in huge furnaces.*

fu|sion /fyuʒən/

ENERGY, THERMODYNAMICS AND HEAT TRANSFER

NOUN **Fusion** is a nuclear reaction in which energy is generated when atoms join together.

○ *Nuclear fusion is difficult to use for the generation of power because a great deal of energy needs to be put in before the atoms will join.*
○ *Controlled nuclear fusion has long been seen as the ultimate energy source of the future.*

Gg

gage or gauge /geɪdʒ/ (gages)

CONTROL, INSTRUMENTATION AND METROLOGY

NOUN A **gage** is an instrument for measuring a quantity. There are many different types of gages.

○ The temperature gage read 170 degrees.

○ Steam boilers must have a pressure gage that indicates the boiler pressure at all times.

gal|van|ic cor|ro|sion /gælvænɪk kərouʒᵊn/

MATERIALS

NOUN **Galvanic corrosion** is a type of corrosion caused by bringing together two different metals, one of which corrodes more rapidly than it would alone while the other corrodes less rapidly.

○ An example of galvanic corrosion is the rusting of iron nails used to hold copper sheet to the bottom of a wooden boat.

○ Galvanic corrosion between the steel fiber and aluminum governs the corrosion behavior of these composites.

gas|ket /gæskɪt/ (gaskets)

MACHINERY AND COMPONENTS

NOUN A **gasket** is a piece of paper, rubber, or other material that can be pressed between the faces or flanges of a joint to provide a seal.

○ Pipe and fittings are bolted together by flanges with a gasket sandwiched between them to provide an airtight joint.

○ A gasket is a mechanical seal that fills the space between two objects, usually to prevent leakage between the two objects while under compression.

gas tur|bine /gæs tɜrbɪn/ (**gas turbines**)

ENERGY, THERMODYNAMICS AND HEAT TRANSFER

NOUN A **gas turbine** is a type of engine in which a shaft is made to rotate by burning gas moving past arrays of blades arranged in circles.

○ *Gas turbines are used to propel aircraft and ships.*

○ *In a gas turbine, a pressurized gas spins the turbine.*

gate valve /geɪt vælv/ (**gate valves**)

FLUID ENGINEERING

NOUN A **gate valve** is a valve with a sliding plate that controls the flow of fluid in a pipe or channel.

○ *Gate valves are usually operated using a handwheel which turns a screw to lift or lower the gate.*

○ *Gate valves contain a sliding disk that moves vertically, perpendicular to the path of the fluid flow.*

gear /ɡɪər/ (**gears**)

MACHINERY AND COMPONENTS

NOUN A **gear** is a wheel with teeth that engage with the teeth of another wheel in order to change the speed or direction of transmitted rotational motion.

○ *Neutral is the position when no gears are engaged and the engine is decoupled from the vehicle's drive wheels.*

○ *The purpose of the gears is to allow the cyclist's legs to move at their optimum rate, no matter how fast the bicycle wheels are moving.*

gear|ing /ɡɪərɪŋ/

MACHINERY AND COMPONENTS

NOUN **Gearing** is an assembly of gears designed to transmit motion.

○ *Four-speed manual gearing used to be standard in British cars.*

○ *The transmission contains a number of different sets of gearing that can be changed to allow a wide range of vehicle speeds.*

ge|o|ther|mal en|er|gy /dʒioʊθɜrmᵊl ɛnərdʒi/

ENERGY, THERMODYNAMICS AND HEAT TRANSFER

NOUN **Geothermal energy** is energy from temperature differences inside the earth's crust.

○ Geothermal energy can be harnessed from volcanoes.

○ In order to extract geothermal energy, it is necessary to efficiently transfer heat from a geothermal reservoir to a power plant, where electrical energy is converted from heat.

gland /glænd/ (glands)

FLUID ENGINEERING

NOUN A **gland** is a device that stops a fluid leaking along a rotating shaft or reciprocating rod passing through a boundary between areas of high and low pressure.

○ The gland in the head of the faucet prevents water from leaking up the shaft when the faucet is turned on.

○ When the packing is compressed by a gland, it provides a tight seal around the stem.

glass /glæs/

MATERIALS

NOUN **Glass** is a type of ceramic with a less ordered molecular structure, usually caused by rapidly cooling it from a molten state.

○ Glass is an amorphous material often, but not always, derived from molten silica.

○ There is a tiny glass window that allows you to see into the furnace.

gov|er|nor /gʌvərnər/ (governors)

MACHINERY AND COMPONENTS

NOUN A **governor** is a device that controls the speed of an engine.

○ Fly-ball governors are used to maintain constant speed in a flywheel.

○ Diesel engines with traditional mechanical injector systems have an integral governor which prevents over-speeding the engine.

grab /græb/ (grabs)

MACHINERY AND COMPONENTS

NOUN A **grab** is a device for gripping and lifting objects, especially the hinged jaws of a mechanical excavator.

○ *An excavator with a huge grab was moving soil.*

○ *The slabs are handled by a hydraulic grab which stacks the slabs as close as a foot apart.*

grind|ing /graɪndɪŋ/

MANUFACTURING AND ASSEMBLY

NOUN **Grinding** is the process of removing the surface of a hard material using a wheel made from or covered in hard grit.

○ *Once the steel had been hardened it was finished by grinding.*

○ *Grinding is done between two disks, one of which is stationary and the other revolving at high speed.*

grind|ing wheel /graɪndɪŋ wil/ (grinding wheels)

MANUFACTURING AND ASSEMBLY

NOUN A **grinding wheel** is a wheel made from or covered in hard grit used for removing the surface of a hard material.

○ *The grinding wheel on a grinding machine should be replaced when it is worn down.*

○ *The performance of grinding wheels and quality of the finished workpiece is affected by how fast the abrasive grains sweep over the workpiece.*

grom|met /grɒmɪt/ (grommets)

MACHINERY AND COMPONENTS

NOUN A **grommet** is a ring of rubber, plastic, or metal put inside a hole to prevent a cable or pipe passing through it from tearing on the sharp edges of the hole.

○ *If any wires have to pass through a sheet metal panel, use a rubber grommet to prevent abrasion.*

○ *An example of a grommet is in a reinforced metal eyelet found in banners used to receive cords or other fasteners.*

ground /graʊnd/

MANUFACTURING AND ASSEMBLY

ADJECTIVE A **ground** object has had its surface finished, its thickness reduced, or its edge sharpened by grinding.

○ *After grinding, there may be marks on the ground surface that only become visible after it has been polished.*

○ *The accuracy of a ground workpiece depends on the profile of the grinding wheel.*

guide /gaɪd/ (guides)

MACHINERY AND COMPONENTS

NOUN A **guide** is a device that directs the motion of a tool or machine part.

○ *The saw has a blade guide to restrain and control the free end of the blade.*

○ *These dies have guides which keep them square when starting the screwing of the pipe.*

guil|lo|tine /gɪlətin/ (guillotines)

MANUFACTURING AND ASSEMBLY

NOUN A **guillotine** is a device for cutting paper, sheet metal, or other sheet materials. It consists of a blade that is brought down onto the sheet.

○ *After the fiberglass is removed from the mold the edges are trimmed with a guillotine.*

○ *A guillotine is useful for cutting stacks of paper.*

gun /gʌn/ (guns)

MANUFACTURING AND ASSEMBLY

NOUN A **gun** is a device used to project something under pressure.

○ *A typical spray gun might apply 10 ounces of paint per minute.*

○ *Sealants are commonly sold in a caulking gun.*

Hh

hard|en|a|bil|i|ty /hɑːrdᵊnəbɪlɪti/

MATERIALS

NOUN The **hardenability** of steel is how easily it can be hardened when cooled rapidly from a high temperature.

○ The steel cracked during welding because its hardenability was too high.

○ In a ferrous alloy, hardenability is the property that determines the depth and distribution of hardness induced by quenching.

> **WORD BUILDER**
> **-ability** = possible
>
> The suffix **-ability** appears in several words that refer to how possible it is to do a particular thing: **machinability**, **weldability**, **workability**.

hard|ness /hɑːrdnɪs/

MATERIALS

NOUN The **hardness** of a material is how strong or resistant to wear it is, measured by indenting the material's surface with a fixed force and measuring the size of the impression made.

○ The steel can be supplied in a range of hardness, depending upon its heat treatment.

○ Hardness is a measure of the resistance of a material to surface indentation or abrasion.

head /hɛd/

FLUID ENGINEERING

NOUN **Head** is a measure of pressure, which is based on the height of a column of liquid.

○ As water in the column pipe fills, air is released through an air release valve and the head builds to a sufficient level above atmospheric pressure.

○ Head is a measure of pressure at a given point in a water system, or the height of a column of water that would produce the pressure.

head|er /hɛdər/ (headers)

FLUID ENGINEERING

NOUN A **header** is a tank that stops the pressure in an apparatus from becoming too great.

○ The header protects the heating system from overpressure.

○ The pressure in the steam header signals the firing controls for the boiler.

heat /hit/

ENERGY, THERMODYNAMICS AND HEAT TRANSFER

NOUN **Heat** is a type of energy associated with temperature.

○ When heat goes into a substance, the temperature of that substance rises.

○ The furnace keeps trying to turn on but then shuts itself off without ever producing any heat.

heat|er /hitər/ (heaters)

ENERGY, THERMODYNAMICS AND HEAT TRANSFER

NOUN A **heater** is a device for supplying heat, for example a radiator or a convector.

○ These water heaters heat water only when it is needed.

○ Turn on the heater and the interior of the car will soon warm up.

WORD BUILDER

-er = do

The suffix **-er** often appears in words for devices, pieces of equipment or substances that carry out a particular function: **atomizer**, **boiler**, **feeder**, **follower**.

---

heat pump /hiːt pʌmp/ (heat pumps)

ENERGY, THERMODYNAMICS AND HEAT TRANSFER

NOUN A **heat pump** is a device for taking heat from a place and delivering it to another place at a much higher temperature.

○ The heat pump transforms thermal energy at a low temperature into thermal energy at a higher temperature.

○ The point at which no more heat can be pulled from the heat source depends on the type of heat pump.

---

heat trans|fer /hiːt trænsfər/

ENERGY, THERMODYNAMICS AND HEAT TRANSFER

NOUN **Heat transfer** is the movement of heat from one substance or material to another.

○ Heat transfer takes place through three principal mechanisms: conduction, radiation, and convection.

○ The primary means of heat transfer in a fired heater are radiation and convection.

---

hel|i|cal gear /hɛlɪkəl gɪər/ (helical gears)

MACHINERY AND COMPONENTS

NOUN **Helical gears** are cylindrical gears with teeth that are at an angle to the axis of rotation of the gear wheel.

○ Helical gears are widely used in gearboxes because of their smooth engagement when the gears are changed.

○ Helical gears are more complex to make but are much better suited for high-speed applications since the teeth engage more gradually than other gears.

hinge /hɪndʒ/ (hinges)

MACHINERY AND COMPONENTS

NOUN A **hinge** is a device consisting of two interlocking metal pieces held by a pin around which they pivot.

○ One half of the hinge is welded to the door pillar, and the other half welded to the door, so that it does not come loose with repeated opening and closing of the door.

○ The lid of the box is connected to the base by hinges.

hon|ing /hoʊnɪŋ/

MANUFACTURING AND ASSEMBLY

NOUN **Honing** is a machining process in which an abrasive cutting tool is used to produce a very fine surface.

○ The final smooth profile of the bore was produced by honing with a fine stone.

○ Honing is done with rigid mounted adjustable stones, and is used to make the bore more accurate than boring can.

hop|per /hɒpər/ (hoppers)

MANUFACTURING AND ASSEMBLY

NOUN A **hopper** is a funnel-shaped container from which solid materials can be emptied into a container below.

○ The fuel goes into a hopper, which has a hole in the bottom through which it can be fed into the furnace below.

○ The clay or cement is poured into a hopper from where it empties it into a tank to be mixed with water or other liquids.

hose /hoʊz/ (hoses)

FLUID ENGINEERING

NOUN A **hose** is a flexible pipe for carrying a liquid or gas.

○ The water is connected to the faucet by a length of rubber hose.

○ Water sprays out like water from a garden hose.

hot work|ing /hɒt wɜrkɪŋ/

MANUFACTURING AND ASSEMBLY

NOUN **Hot working** is a process in which a metal is shaped under pressure at a fairly high temperature.

○ Hot working of this material may be done in the temperature range of 2150 F to 1800 F.

○ Hot working improves the engineering properties of the workpiece because it replaces the microstructure with one that has fine spherical shaped grains.

> **RELATED WORDS**
>
> Compare **hot working** with **cold working**, a process in which metal is shaped at a fairly low temperature. **Cold working** increases the metal's **yield strength** but makes it less **ductile**.

hous|ing /haʊzɪŋ/ (housings)

MACHINERY AND COMPONENTS

NOUN A **housing** is a part designed to cover, contain, or support a component or mechanism.

○ The bearing is contained in a cast iron housing.

○ The crown wheel, pinion, and differential assembly is enclosed in a housing.

hub /hʌb/ (hubs)

MACHINERY AND COMPONENTS

NOUN A **hub** is the central part of something such as a wheel, propeller, or fan, through which the axle passes.

○ The axle passes through the hub of the wheel.

○ Blades project from the hub of the propeller and propel the boat in the direction of travel.

hunt /hʌnt/ (hunts, hunted, hunting)

MACHINERY AND COMPONENTS

VERB If something, for example engine speed, **hunts**, it keeps going up and down around a mean value or position.

○ A governor is said to hunt if the speed of the engine fluctuates continuously above and below the mean speed.

○ Stability is the ability of a governor to maintain engine speed without hunting.

---

hy|drau|lic /haɪdrɒlɪk/

FLUID ENGINEERING

ADJECTIVE **Hydraulic** parts or machines are operated by pressure transmitted through a pipe by a liquid.

○ The grab on the tractor would not work because the hydraulic fluid had leaked from the cylinder.

○ In a hydraulic system, force that is applied at one point is transmitted to another point using an incompressible fluid.

> **WORD BUILDER**
> **hydr-/hydro-** = relating to water
>
> The prefix **hydr-** or **hydro-** appears in several words that relate to water or another liquid: **hydraulic press**, **hydraulic ram**, **hydrostatic pressure**.

---

hy|drau|lic press /haɪdrɒlɪk prɛs/ (**hydraulic presses**)

MANUFACTURING AND ASSEMBLY

NOUN A **hydraulic press** is a press that uses liquid pressure to make a small force applied to a small piston produce a large force on a larger piston.

○ A hydraulic press produces a great deal of force from the application of a small amount of force to the small piston.

○ A hydraulic press applies pressure of about 2500 psi between the second pressure-bonding plate and the pressure-bonding die.

---

hy|drau|lic ram /haɪdrɒlɪk ræm/ (**hydraulic rams**)

FLUID ENGINEERING

NOUN A **hydraulic ram** is a large device in which a piston or plunger is displaced by the pressure of a fluid.

○ A hydraulic ram is a sealed cylinder attached to a piston. When oil flows into one side of the cylinder, it pushes the piston up.

○ A hydraulic ram was used to raise the front end of the car.

---

hy|dro|stat|ic pres|sure /haɪdrəstætɪk prɛʃər/

FLUID ENGINEERING

NOUN **Hydrostatic pressure** is the pressure exerted by a liquid that depends on how deep it is.

○ As the car began to sink, the hydrostatic pressure of the water made it impossible to open the doors.

○ The hydrostatic pressure of fresh water is 0.433 pounds per square inch per foot of depth.

i|dle /ˈaɪdəl/ (idles, idled, idling)

GENERAL

VERB If an engine or shaft **idles**, it turns without doing anything useful, for example moving a vehicle forward or making another part move.

○ Let the engine idle for a few minutes after coming to a stop, then shut it down and let it cool.

○ A control program puts the car in neutral when it is idling, even when the gear selector is in another position.

im|pact /ˈɪmpækt/

GENERAL

NOUN Impact is the sudden application of a force.

○ The tool assembly includes a shock absorber to absorb impact from the work tool at the end of a stroke.

○ The impact of the hammer on the nail is felt through a pressure on the palm of the hand.

im|pulse /ˈɪmpʌls/ (impulses)

MECHANICS AND DYNAMICS

NOUN If an **impulse** is applied to an object, a force acts on it which lasts for a particular period of time.

○ When a bat hits a ball, an impulse is applied to the ball because the bat puts a force on the ball for a short time.

○ Forces applied over time create impulses.

in|com|press|i|ble /ɪnkəmprɛsɪbᵊl/

GENERAL

ADJECTIVE **Incompressible** fluids and solids will not change in volume if a pressure is applied to them.

○ Water is not incompressible – it reduces in volume by around 0.5 percent per 1,000 psi of pressure.

○ Solid matter is rigid, has a fixed shape, and is incompressible.

in|dex /ɪndɛks/ (indexes, indexed, indexing)

MANUFACTURING AND ASSEMBLY

VERB To **index** a machine or a workpiece held in a machine tool means to move it so that one particular operation will be repeated at particular intervals.

○ Workpieces can be indexed for a number of different cuts that are at an angle to each other.

○ The faceplate is indexed in 1 degree increments around the whole plate.

in|er|tia /ɪnɜrʃə/

MECHANICS AND DYNAMICS

NOUN **Inertia** is the resistance of a body to being moved.

○ A block of iron has greater inertia than a block of wood of the same shape and size.

○ The turbo may keep on spinning for a few more seconds if the engine was racing just before being switched off, simply because of inertia.

in|got /ɪŋgət/ (ingots)

GENERAL

NOUN An **ingot** is an unfinished cast piece of metal.

○ Steel ingots are blocks of steel ready to be rolled or melted.

○ Forging involves using hard blows to form and shape metallic ingots into useful items.

in|let /ˈɪnlɛt/ (**inlets**)

FLUID ENGINEERING

NOUN An **inlet** is a tube, valve, or other part through which a fluid enters a device or machine.

○ Gas flows steadily in through the inlet and out through the outlet.

○ The inlet at the base of the windshield allows outside air to enter the air-conditioning system.

in|stru|men|ta|tion /ˌɪnstrəmɛnˈteɪʃᵊn/

GENERAL

NOUN **Instrumentation** consists of a set of sensors and electronic apparatus for measuring or monitoring a process.

○ The paper describes the state of the development of these sensors and measuring systems and shows examples of measurements made with this instrumentation.

○ Reconnect the instrumentation to a second sensor for the test material measurements.

in|su|la|tion /ˌɪnsəˈleɪʃᵊn/

ENERGY, THERMODYNAMICS AND HEAT TRANSFER

NOUN **Insulation** is put on or around a container or pipe to stop heat from being lost.

○ Put some insulation around the tank to prevent heat escaping from it.

○ If more insulation is used, less heat is lost from the pipe.

in|take /ˈɪnteɪk/ (intakes)

FLUID ENGINEERING

NOUN An **intake** is an opening through which fluid enters a duct or channel, usually the air inlet of an engine.

○ It is important to ensure that solid objects do not enter the air intake of the jet engine.

○ Most vehicles have air intake systems that regulate the temperature of the air entering the engine.

in|te|gral /ˈɪntɪɡrəl/

CONTROL, INSTRUMENTATION AND METROLOGY

ADJECTIVE An **integral** control is a type of control where the strength of the output is adjusted according to all the differences from the setpoint that have been recorded since the beginning of a process.

○ Integral control in a process control system will integrate (add up) any differences between the measurement and the setpoint in order to ensure that these are minimized over time.

○ The major advantage of integral controllers is that they can return the controlled variable back to the exact setpoint following a disturbance.

in|ter|fer|om|e|ter /ˌɪntərfərˈɒmɪtər/ (interferometers)

CONTROL, INSTRUMENTATION AND METROLOGY

NOUN An **interferometer** is an instrument that measures distance by seeing how light waves combine.

○ Most interferometers use light or some other form of electromagnetic wave to measure distance.

○ An interferometer is an instrument used to measure waves through interference patterns.

in|vest|ment cast|ing /ɪnˈvɛstmənt ˈkæstɪŋ/

MANUFACTURING AND ASSEMBLY

NOUN **Investment casting** is a casting process in which a mold is made around a wax pattern that is burned away when the molten material is poured in.

○ In investment casting, a ceramic slurry is applied around a disposable pattern to form a mold.

○ Lost-foam casting is a casting process that is similar to investment casting except foam is used for the pattern instead of wax.

---

in|vis|cid /ɪnˈvɪsɪd/

FLUID ENGINEERING

ADJECTIVE An **inviscid** flow is a type of flow in which viscous forces are very small in comparison with inertial ones.

○ In large-bore pipes the flow can often be assumed to be inviscid.

○ Bernoulli's principle states that, for an inviscid flow, an increase in the speed of the fluid occurs simultaneously with a decrease in pressure or a decrease in the fluid's potential energy.

> **OTHER TYPES OF FLOW INCLUDE:**
>
> irrotational, laminar, steady-state, turbulent

---

ir|re|vers|i|ble /ɪrɪˈvɜrsɪbəl/

ENERGY, THERMODYNAMICS AND HEAT TRANSFER

ADJECTIVE An **irreversible** thermodynamic process cannot happen in the reverse direction without changing the surroundings.

○ The best-known example of an irreversible process is the flow of heat, which can only take place from a warmer area to a cooler one.

○ Many thermodynamic processes are irreversible.

---

ir|ro|ta|tio|nal /ɪroʊˈteɪʃənəl/

FLUID ENGINEERING

ADJECTIVE An **irrotational** flow does not contain vortices.

○ As the water passed under the bridge, its flow changed from being irrotational to having many vortices in the wake of the columns.

○ Irrotational flow means that the fluid elements may deform but cannot rotate.

i|so|la|tion /aɪsəleɪʃᵊn/

MECHANICS AND DYNAMICS

NOUN **Isolation** of a machine or structure involves the use of supports that absorb vibrations to reduce the vibrations that are transmitted to or from it.

○ *Isolation of the machine is very important, as it will localize the disturbing influences of the machinery.*

○ *The isolation of buildings from ground motion by means of rubber bearings is common in some earthquake zones.*

I

jack|et /dʒækɪt/ (jackets)

MACHINERY AND COMPONENTS

NOUN A **jacket** is a cover or casing for the outside of something, for example the insulating cover of a boiler.

○ *The bullet has a metal jacket that encloses a lead alloy core.*

○ *Ensure that the hot water cylinder has an insulating jacket with no gaps around it.*

jaw /dʒɔ/ (jaws)

MANUFACTURING AND ASSEMBLY

NOUN The **jaws** of a machine or tool are a pair of hinged or sliding components designed to grip a workpiece.

○ *The workpiece is mounted between the moveable jaws of the vise.*

○ *Bolt cutters have a pair of opposing jaws that cut with a pinching action.*

jig /dʒɪg/ (jigs)

MANUFACTURING AND ASSEMBLY

NOUN A **jig** is a device for holding and supporting a workpiece in a machine tool and for guiding the cutting tool.

○ *Jigs are similar to fixtures, but they not only locate and hold the part but also guide the cutting tools.*

○ *A simple machining jig was used to ensure the assembly could be accurately lined up.*

jour|nal /dʒɜːnəl/ (journals)

NOUN The **journal** of a shaft or axle is the part of it that is in contact with or enclosed by a bearing.

○ *The journal of the shaft (the part in contact with the bearing) slides over the bearing surface.*

○ *If a main bearing has suffered wear then the journal supported by the bearing will take up a lower position.*

J

Kk

---

key|way /ˈkiːweɪ/ (keyways)

MACHINERY AND COMPONENTS

NOUN A **keyway** is a long slot cut into a component to accept a key that engages with a similar slot on a mating component so that the two components do not move against each other.

○ If the key is not fitting properly in both the flywheel and crank shaft keyways, replace the key.

○ A keyway is a slot or groove in which a key slides.

---

kin|e|mat|ics /ˌkɪnɪˈmætɪks/

MANUFACTURING AND ASSEMBLY

NOUN **Kinematics** is the study of the movement of objects or of groups of objects.

○ Kinematics is important in the design of robots and machine tools.

○ Kinematics is the branch of mechanics that deals with the motion of bodies without reference to the cause or force producing it.

---

ki|net|ic en|er|gy /kɪˈnɛtɪk ˈɛnərdʒi/

MECHANICS AND DYNAMICS

NOUN **Kinetic energy** is the energy that a body contains because of its mass and speed.

○ The device converts kinetic energy from the movement of the wind, ocean, or river currents into useful mechanical power.

○ When the electrons strike the workpiece, their kinetic energy changes to heat, which vaporizes minute amounts of the material.

knuck|le joint /nʌkᵊl dʒɔɪnt/ (**knuckle joints**)

MACHINERY AND COMPONENTS

NOUN A **knuckle joint** is a hinged joint between two rods, often a ball and socket joint.

○ Knuckle joints are used to connect two rods when some degree of flexibility or angular movement is needed.

○ By using knuckle joints, the light fittings are able to be turned so that light can be shone in any direction.

K

Ll

lam|i|nar /ˈlæmɪnər/

FLUID ENGINEERING

ADJECTIVE A **laminar** flow takes place in layers without interaction between them, so that all parts move in one direction.

- ○ Laminar flow over the wing of an aircraft is the smooth flow of air molecules over its surface.
- ○ In laminar flow, layers of water flow over one another at different speeds with virtually no mixing between layers.

la|ser /ˈleɪzər/ (**lasers**)

GENERAL

NOUN A **laser** is a device for producing a beam of light that can measure things or heat things at very high temperatures.

- ○ Lasers allow energy to be released in very short time intervals, and their beams can be focused on very small spots.
- ○ The scanner uses a laser to find a set of 3D points that define the object's shape.

la|ser ma|chin|ing /ˈleɪzər məˈʃiːnɪŋ/

MANUFACTURING AND ASSEMBLY

NOUN **Laser machining** is a process in which material is removed from a surface using light from a laser.

- ○ The very small holes in the aircraft wing could be made more efficiently by laser machining than by drilling.
- ○ In laser machining, the metal is cut by melting and vaporizing it with an intense beam of light from a laser.

lathe /leɪð/ (**lathes**)

MANUFACTURING AND ASSEMBLY

NOUN A **lathe** is a machine tool in which the workpiece is rotated relative to a cutting tool.

○ *The lathe makes parts by spinning the part and using a cutting tool to take material off it.*

○ *Examples of parts that can be produced on a lathe are crankshafts, camshafts, and bearing mounts.*

> **LATHE PARTS MAY INCLUDE:**
>
> carriage, center, chuck, faceplate, spindle

lay|up /leɪʌp/

MANUFACTURING AND ASSEMBLY

NOUN **Layup** of a composite structure involves arranging the dry components before pouring in a liquid which will set hard.

○ *The simplest technique for making a composite structure uses manual placement of the fibers and is called layup.*

○ *Many composite layup designs use a sandwich structure.*

lev|er /lɪvər/ (**levers**)

GENERAL

NOUN A **lever** is a rigid bar pivoted around a fulcrum, used to transfer a force to a load and usually to provide a mechanical advantage.

○ *A crowbar is an example of a lever because it helps to lift heavy objects.*

○ *The hand brake is usually applied by a lever at the side of the driver's seat.*

lin|er /laɪnər/ (**liners**)

MACHINERY AND COMPONENTS

NOUN A **liner** is a sleeve that will withstand wear or corrosion, fixed inside or outside a structural component or container.

○ *Textile liners fixed inside the wheel arches help reduce tire noise.*

○ *Install the proper size bearing liners (inserts) to bring the clearance to standard.*

---

link /lɪŋk/ (links)

MACHINERY AND COMPONENTS

NOUN A **link** is a connecting piece in a mechanism, often with pivoted ends.

○ *Individual links are connected together to form a chain.*

○ *One type of conveyer is a carrier belt structure made from pivotally interconnected rigid links.*

---

link|age /lɪŋkɪdʒ/ (linkages)

MACHINERY AND COMPONENTS

NOUN A **linkage** is a system of connected levers or rods for transmitting or regulating a mechanism's motion.

○ *The steering linkage is the system that connects the steering wheel to the front wheels and allows the wheels to change direction in response to commands from the driver.*

○ *The top link of the three-point linkage is attached to a spring loaded lever which is pushed forward by the top link as the implement begins work.*

---

live steam /laɪv stim/

ENERGY, THERMODYNAMICS AND HEAT TRANSFER

NOUN **Live steam** is steam supplied directly from a boiler at full pressure.

○ *An escape of live steam from a boiler can be extremely dangerous.*

○ *The valve is used to allow live steam into the feedwater heater when exhaust steam is not available.*

---

lock|nut /lɒknʌt/ (locknuts)

MACHINERY AND COMPONENTS

NOUN A **locknut** is an extra nut screwed down on another nut to stop it from shaking loose.

○ *Because the joint is subject to vibration the nut needs first to be tightened and then a locknut applied to ensure that it does not shake loose.*

○ *Lock the adjusting bolt with the locknut and check the clearance again.*

---

lu|bri|ca|tion /luːbrɪkeɪʃən/

FLUID ENGINEERING

NOUN **Lubrication** involves adding a substance between solid surfaces that are moving against each other in order to reduce friction and wear.

○ *It is important to use a good-quality grease for lubrication of the bearings.*

○ *The basic purpose of lubrication is to minimize friction and wear.*

Mm

ma|chin|a|bil|i|ty /məʃinəbɪlɪti/

NOUN The **machinability** of a material is how easily it can be machined using a cutting tool.

- A material is said to have good machinability if tool wear is low and the surface finish produced is good.
- The high chemical reactivity of the material with many tool materials and the low elastic modulus contribute to its difficult machinability.

ma|chine /məʃin/ (**machines, machined, machining**)

VERB If you **machine** a workpiece, you shape it, cut it, or remove material from it using a machine tool.

- Grinding is the most expensive way of machining metal.
- On this model the ram can get very close to the workpiece, which is an advantage when machining very thin workpieces.

ma|chine tool /məʃin tul/ (**machine tools**)

NOUN A **machine tool** is a power-driven machine, for example a lathe, miller, or grinder, that is used for cutting, shaping, and finishing materials.

- They sell lathes, grinders, and other machine tools.
- A lathe is a type of machine tool which can be used for shaping metal or wood.

m

ma|chin|ing /məʃinɪŋ/

MANUFACTURING AND ASSEMBLY

NOUN Machining is the process of cutting, shaping, or removing material from a workpiece using a machine tool.

○ *All our machining is done on the highest quality machine tools.*

○ *A reamer is a tool used in machining to make existing holes more accurate.*

> **COMPARE THESE OTHER CUTTING AND SHAPING PROCESSES:**
>
> drilling, honing, milling, reaming, turning

male /meɪl/

GENERAL

ADJECTIVE A **male** component has a projecting part that fits into a part on another component.

○ *The (external) male thread on the pipe makes a connection with the mating female (internal) thread.*

○ *The coupling is threaded on the inside so only a male connection can be joined to it.*

man|drel /mændrəl/ (**mandrels**)

MANUFACTURING AND ASSEMBLY

NOUN A **mandrel** is a spindle for supporting a workpiece when it is being machined.

○ *Conical and curved parts can be made by spinning them on a rotating mandrel.*

○ *A mandrel is a workholder for turning that fits the inner diameter of workpieces.*

ma|nip|u|la|tor /mənɪpyʊleɪtər/ (**manipulators**)

CONTROL, INSTRUMENTATION AND METROLOGY

NOUN A **manipulator** is a type of actuator which is used to move objects in a similar way to a human hand.

○ *The user controls a robotic manipulator and makes it pick up a target object.*

○ *Some robot manipulators are controlled using methods that do not take into account the flexibility of the links and joints.*

---

ma|nom|e|ter /mənɒmɪtər/ (**manometers**)

CONTROL, INSTRUMENTATION AND METROLOGY

NOUN A **manometer** is an instrument, usually consisting of a tube with an open end, which measures pressure differences between different points in a fluid.

○ *The pressure of the system is measured with an open-end manometer.*

○ *Pressure was once commonly measured by its ability to displace a column of liquid in a manometer.*

---

man|u|fac|ture /mænyəfæktʃər/

GENERAL

NOUN The **manufacture** of goods or products is the process of making them.

○ *Limestone is used in the manufacture of glass.*

○ *CHO is important in the manufacture of numerous products, such as paper, textiles, and explosives.*

---

mas|ter cyl|in|der /mæstər sɪlɪndər/ (**master cylinders**)

MACHINERY AND COMPONENTS

NOUN The **master cylinder** in a hydraulic system is a large cylinder in which the working fluid is compressed by a piston so it can drive one or more other cylinders.

○ *The heart of the brake system is the master cylinder, which controls the hydraulic pressure of the entire system.*

○ *The master cylinder uses two pistons in the same cylinder to supply pressure to both brake circuits in the car.*

me|chan|i|cal ad|van|tage /mɪkænɪkᵊl ædvæntɪdʒ/

GENERAL

NOUN **Mechanical advantage** is a measure of how much a force is increased by using a tool or machine. It is equal to the force exerted by the tool or machine divided by the applied effort.

○ A long lever with a fulcrum near to one end offers a better mechanical advantage than a shorter one, or one with a fulcrum nearer the middle.

○ In caliper brakes, the long distance from the pivot to the pad reduces mechanical advantage and allows the arms to flex, reducing braking effectiveness.

me|chan|i|cal test|ing /mɪkænɪkᵊl tɛstɪŋ/

MECHANICS AND DYNAMICS

NOUN **Mechanical testing** is the testing of a material to find out its mechanical properties, for example its yield strength or hardness.

○ Mechanical testing is used to ensure that supplied materials will perform as expected.

○ Mechanical testing of materials covers a wide variety of experimental approaches, ranging from a simple standard tensile test to more complex tests.

me|chan|ics /mɪkænɪks/

GENERAL

NOUN **Mechanics** involves how bodies or parts of bodies work together because of the forces that are applied between them.

○ Dynamics is the branch of mechanics that studies bodies in motion.

○ In principle, it is possible to study the mechanics of a fluid by studying the motion of the molecules themselves.

mech|a|nism /mɛkənɪzəm/ (**mechanisms**)

MACHINERY AND COMPONENTS

NOUN A **mechanism** is a system or structure of moving parts that performs a particular function, especially in a machine.

○A chain drive is a mechanism consisting of a chain or chains for transmitting power.

○The steering mechanism that is widely used on cars worldwide is rack-and-pinion.

---

melt|ing /mɛltɪŋ/

ENERGY, THERMODYNAMICS AND HEAT TRANSFER

NOUN **Melting** is the action of changing from a solid to a liquid as the temperature is raised.

○Melting will not happen until the ice has warmed up to 0 degrees.

○Solder is any alloy used for joining metals that has a low melting point, usually around 200°C.

---

mesh /mɛʃ/ (**meshes, meshed, meshing**)

MACHINERY AND COMPONENTS

VERB If gear teeth **mesh** with other gear teeth, or are **meshed** with them, they fit together and start working together.

○This gear meshes with another gear, which turns the pinion gear shaft.

○Shift all the gears into position and look at how the gear teeth mesh.

---

met|al|lur|gy /mɛtˀlɜrdʒi/

GENERAL

NOUN **Metallurgy** is the study of metals and alloys.

○An important part of metallurgy is the production of metals from their ores.

○The metallurgy course will cover metals and alloy systems, iron-carbon alloys, and corrosion and scale resistant alloys.

---

me|trol|o|gy /mɪtrɒlədʒi/

CONTROL, INSTRUMENTATION AND METROLOGY

NOUN **Metrology** is the technology of measuring the dimensions of components.

○ *Metrology includes all aspects of measurement.*

○ *They used coordinate measuring machines, laser inferometers, and other metrology equipment.*

> **WORD BUILDER**
> **-ology** = the study of
>
> The suffix **-ology** forms a noun, meaning "the study of" something: **metrology**, **rheology**, **tribology**.

mi|crom|e|ter /maɪkrɒmɪtər/ (micrometers)

CONTROL, INSTRUMENTATION AND METROLOGY

NOUN A **micrometer** is a device that uses a screw gage to measure components very exactly.

○ *The diameter of very thin wire can be measured accurately with a micrometer.*

○ *A micrometer is a hand-held instrument for accurately measuring small distances, usually thickness or diameter.*

mill /mɪl/ (mills)

MANUFACTURING AND ASSEMBLY

NOUN A **mill** is a machine in which material is ground or crushed into a powder or into very small pieces.

○ *What is the most economical mill for grinding silica rocks into powder?*

○ *The raw ceramic is then crushed in a grinding mill to provide a powder for reinforcing the metal.*

mill|ing /mɪlɪŋ/

MANUFACTURING AND ASSEMBLY

NOUN **Milling** is the process of grinding, cutting, pressing, or crushing a material in a special machine.

○ *Milling is the process of cutting away material by feeding a workpiece past a rotating cutter with many teeth.*

○ *Milling is the complex cutting of metal or other materials by removing material from a planar surface to form the final shape.*

mill|ing ma|chine /mɪlɪŋ məʃin/ (**milling machines**)

MANUFACTURING AND ASSEMBLY

NOUN A **milling machine** is a machine tool in which a horizontal arbor or vertical spindle rotates a cutting tool above a horizontal table, which is used to move a workpiece.

○ A milling machine will shave off small sections of the metal until the final product is produced.

○ A milling machine was used to remove the bulk of the material and a lathe to finish the profile.

mod|al a|nal|y|sis /moʊdᵊl ənælɪsɪs/

MECHANICS AND DYNAMICS

NOUN **Modal analysis** is the analysis of a structure to find its natural frequencies of vibration.

○ Modal analysis is done to determine the vibration characteristics of a structure.

○ It is the task of modal analysis to determine a system's different modes of vibration.

mode /moʊd/ (**modes**)

MECHANICS AND DYNAMICS

NOUN A **mode** is a particular pattern or shape in which a mechanical system will vibrate.

○ Most systems have many modes of vibration.

○ The actual vibration of a structure is a combination of all its different vibration modes.

mod|u|lus of e|las|tic|i|ty /mɒdʒələs əv ɪlæstɪsɪti/

MATERIALS

NOUN The **modulus of elasticity** of a material is a measure of its stiffness. It is equal to the stress applied to it divided by the resulting elastic strain.

○ The modulus of elasticity of steel is many times higher than that of rubber.

○ By definition, a stiffer material has a higher modulus of elasticity.

mold|ing (BRIT moulding) /ˈmoʊldɪŋ/

MANUFACTURING AND ASSEMBLY

NOUN **Molding** is a process in which a molten or liquid material is poured into a mold and allowed to set or freeze.

○ Molding involves shaping molten plastic resins in something called a pattern.

○ The trouble with molding is that when you remove the pattern, some sand breaks away and causes patching.

mo|ment /ˈmoʊmənt/ (moments)

MECHANICS AND DYNAMICS

NOUN A **moment** is the ability of a force to turn, twist, or bend. It is equal to the force multiplied by the distance from the center of twisting, turning, or bending.

○ Using a long-handled wrench allows a greater moment to be applied to the nut.

○ Torque is the moment of force which tends to twist a structure.

mo|ment of in|er|tia /ˈmoʊmənt əv ɪnˈɜrʃə/ (moments of inertia)

MECHANICS AND DYNAMICS

NOUN The **moment of inertia** of the cross-section of a body is its resistance to changes in its rotation. It depends on how far each part of the body's mass is from its center.

○ A flywheel is designed to have a high moment of inertia so that, once spinning, it is difficult to slow down.

○ The moment of inertia is a measure of how resistant an object is to changes in its rotational motion.

mo|men|tum /moʊmɛntəm/

MECHANICS AND DYNAMICS

NOUN The **momentum** of a moving body is its mass multiplied by its velocity.

○ Although the train and the car were moving at the same speed, the momentum of the train was much higher.

○ If too much power is applied to the front brake, the momentum of the rider propels him or her over the handlebars.

mo|tor /moʊtər/ (**motors**)

GENERAL

NOUN A **motor** is a device that changes a form of energy into mechanical energy to produce motion.

○ Electric motors convert electrical energy into mechanical energy.

○ The generator may be driven by a motor connected to the electricity supply.

mul|ti|phase flow /mʌltɪfeɪz floʊ/

FLUID ENGINEERING

NOUN **Multiphase flow** is a type of flow that involves more than one fluid, for example a liquid and a gas, or two liquids that do not mix.

○ Both oil and gas came out of the well, so the engineers had to deal with the problems of multiphase flow.

○ A multiphase flow meter is a device used in the oil and gas industry to measure the individual phase flow rates of petroleum, water and gas mixtures.

m

Nn

nat|u|ral con|vec|tion /nætʃərəl kənvɛkʃ°n/

ENERGY, THERMODYNAMICS AND HEAT TRANSFER

NOUN **Natural convection** is the loss of heat from a hot solid or liquid, without the air around it being moved around by anything or anyone.

- ○ Air that is in contact with a hot plate will carry heat to its surroundings by natural convection.
- ○ When you leave a hot cake to cool on the kitchen counter, the heat transfer is by natural convection.

> **RELATED WORDS**
>
> Compare **natural convection** with **forced convection** in which the movement of fluid does not happen naturally but is helped by a device such as a fan or pump.

nat|u|ral gas /nætʃərəl gæs/

ENERGY, THERMODYNAMICS AND HEAT TRANSFER

NOUN **Natural gas** is a fuel consisting mostly of methane gas, extracted from under the ocean or ground.

- ○ Natural gas contains methane, ethane, propane, and butane and can often be used directly without any processing.
- ○ Methane is the principal component of natural gas.

nav|i|ga|tion sys|tem /nævɪgeɪʃ°n sɪstəm/ (**navigation systems**)

CONTROL, INSTRUMENTATION AND METROLOGY

NOUN A **navigation system** is an instrument that determines the position of a vehicle and the route to a particular place.

○ The car's navigation system tells the driver to turn left or right at a particular junction.

○ The navigation system uses GPS signals to determine the vehicle's current location and direction.

---

nee|dle valve /niːdᵊl vælv/ (needle valves)

FLUID ENGINEERING

NOUN A **needle valve** is a valve containing a narrow pointed rod that can be moved in or out to control the flow of a fluid.

○ The fuel flowed to the engine through a needle valve so that it could be regulated precisely.

○ Needle valves have elongated conically-tapered disks and matching seats for fine flow control.

New|to|ni|an /nutoʊniən/

GENERAL

ADJECTIVE **Newtonian** means relating to the work of Isaac Newton or obeying the laws described by him.

○ Classical mechanics is sometimes still called Newtonian mechanics because it is based on the laws first set out by Isaac Newton.

○ The dynamics of space flight are developed from the Newtonian viewpoint.

---

non-de|struc|tive test|ing (ABBR NDT) /nɒndɪstrʌktɪv testɪŋ/

CONTROL, INSTRUMENTATION AND METROLOGY

NOUN **Non-destructive testing** is the examination of the quality of a component without changing it in any way.

○ With non-destructive testing, you can test a product and get adequate information with the benefit that you still have the product.

○ No amusement ride can be operated unless non-destructive testing of the ride has been done.

nor|mal|iz|ing /nɔːrməlaɪzɪŋ/

MANUFACTURING AND ASSEMBLY

NOUN **Normalizing** is a process in which a metal is heated to a temperature below its melting point and allowed to cool in air in order to make it more ductile.

○ Normalizing is a process in which a metal is cooled in air after being heated in order to relieve stress.

○ Normalizing is often done to remove the stresses in aircraft steels.

noz|zle /nɒzᵊl/ (nozzles)

FLUID ENGINEERING

NOUN A **nozzle** is a narrow pipe, used to control the flow of a fluid as it leaves another pipe.

○ Water is sprayed from nozzles above the condenser.

○ The liquid can be sprayed into a gas stream by means of a nozzle which disperses the liquid into a fine spray of drops.

nu|cle|ar en|er|gy /nuːkliər ɛnərdʒi/

ENERGY, THERMODYNAMICS AND HEAT TRANSFER

NOUN **Nuclear energy** is energy produced from nuclear fission or nuclear fusion.

○ Uranium is a radioactive substance used in the production of nuclear energy.

○ The splitting of the atomic nucleus of a heavy element results in the emission of nuclear energy.

nu|cle|ar re|ac|tor /nuːkliər riæktər/ (nuclear reactors)

ENERGY, THERMODYNAMICS AND HEAT TRANSFER

NOUN A **nuclear reactor** is a container in which nuclear fission or nuclear fusion happens in order to produce energy.

○ Nuclear reactors have systems to close down nuclear fission if unsafe conditions are detected.

○ Fuel rods containing uranium are placed next to each other in a vessel called a nuclear reactor.

nut /nʌt/ (**nuts**)

MACHINERY AND COMPONENTS

NOUN A **nut** is a small square or hexagonal block with a threaded hole through the middle for screwing on the end of a bolt.

○ *Thread a nut onto the bolt to keep it in place.*

○ *We supply all kinds of fastenings including nuts and bolts, screws, and many others.*

n

Oo

o|pen chan|nel /oʊpən tʃænᵊl/ (open channels)

FLUID ENGINEERING

NOUN An **open channel** is a type of flow in which one surface is free (= not restricted by anything).

○ A canal is an example of open channel flow.

○ Open channel flow has a free surface but pipe flow does not.

o|pen-die forg|ing /oʊpən daɪ fɔrdʒɪŋ/

MANUFACTURING AND ASSEMBLY

NOUN **Open-die forging** is a forging process in which the flow of metal is not kept completely in the die.

○ Open-die forging is used only for rough shaping of a billet.

○ Open-die forging gets its name from the fact that the dies do not enclose the workpiece, allowing it to flow except where contacted by the dies.

or|i|fice me|ter /ɔrɪfɪs mitər/ (orifice meters)

CONTROL, INSTRUMENTATION AND METROLOGY

NOUN An **orifice meter** is a device with a hole in it that measures how fast a fluid is flowing by recording the pressure decrease across the hole.

○ The two most important factors that influence the reading of an orifice meter are the size of the orifice and the diameter of the pipe which it is fitted into.

○ The simplest and most common device for measuring flow rate in a pipe is an orifice meter.

out|put /ˈaʊtpʊt/ (**outputs**)

GENERAL

NOUN The **output** of an engine or system is the power, energy, or work it produces.

○ *The maximum power output of an engine occurs when the rate of gas flow is at its maximum.*

○ *Since the voltage is low, the power output of the system is also low.*

Pp

pack /pæk/ (packs, packed, packing)

MANUFACTURING AND ASSEMBLY

VERB If you **pack** a joint, you seal it by adding a layer of compressible material between the two parts.

○ You can't pack the joint with cement if there isn't a firm back to it.

○ Having the joints packed with the correct grease will reduce friction, reduce wear and help minimize water ingress.

pack|ing /pækɪŋ/

FLUID ENGINEERING

NOUN **Packing** is a substance or material used to completely seal joints so that no gas or liquid can escape from them.

○ Insert some packing into the joints to make them watertight.

○ They tried to stop the leak by pressing packing into the joint.

par|ti|cle kin|e|mat|ics /pɑrtɪkᵊl kɪnɪmætɪks/

MECHANICS AND DYNAMICS

NOUN **Particle kinematics** is the study of the movement of particles, without considering the forces that cause this movement.

○ Since the forces causing the motion of the dust particles are not under direct control, it is appropriate to study their motion using particle kinematics.

○ A special case of particle kinematics that occurs frequently is that of a particle sliding while in continuous contact with a surface.

par|ti|cle ki|net|ics /pɑrtɪkᵊl kɪnɛtɪks/

MECHANICS AND DYNAMICS

NOUN **Particle kinetics** is the study of the movement of particles and the forces that cause this movement.

- ○ The motions of the balls in a game of pool can be analyzed using particle kinetics because the forces that cause motion are under control.

- ○ As in particle kinematics, in particle kinetics you need to consider only the translational motion of the particle.

pawl /pɔl/ (**pawls**)

MACHINERY AND COMPONENTS

NOUN A **pawl** is a pivoted lever shaped to engage with a ratchet wheel to prevent motion in a particular direction.

- ○ A parking pawl prevents the transmission from rotating, and therefore the vehicle from moving.

- ○ A pawl engages with notches on the lower edge of the horizontal bar, which prevent the bar from being moved back until it has been-drawn fully forwards.

phase /feɪz/ (**phases**)

ENERGY, THERMODYNAMICS AND HEAT TRANSFER

NOUN A **phase** of a substance is whether it is a solid, liquid, or gas, and its chemical composition at a particular time.

- ○ A phase change (liquid to solid) is involved when water freezes.
- ○ The working fluid is in its liquid phase at this point.

pho|to|vol|ta|ic /foʊtoʊvɔlteɪɪk/

ENERGY, THERMODYNAMICS AND HEAT TRANSFER

ADJECTIVE A **photovoltaic** device produces a voltage when it is exposed to light.

- ○ Special panels of photovoltaic cells capture light from the sun and convert it into electricity.

- ○ A solar cell is a photovoltaic device that produces an electrical current from light.

p

P|I|D /piː aɪ diː/

CONTROL, INSTRUMENTATION AND METROLOGY

ABBREVIATION A **PID** is a type of controller that uses proportional, integral, and differential control.

○ *A PID controller uses information about present, past, and future errors to adjust a process.*

○ *The diagram shows a closed-loop system controlled by a PID.*

pi|lot /paɪlət/ (**pilots**)

MANUFACTURING AND ASSEMBLY

NOUN A **pilot** is a guide used to help join two mating parts together.

○ *A pilot can be inserted into a drill chuck to guide the drill bit.*

○ *Drill a pilot hole to make it easier to drive a nail or screw into the wall.*

Pi|tot tube /piːtoʊ tub/ (**Pitot tubes**)

CONTROL, INSTRUMENTATION AND METROLOGY

NOUN A **Pitot tube** is a device for measuring pressure in a fluid. This term is named for French engineer Henri Pitot (1695–1771).

○ *The airspeed of the glider was measured using a Pitot tube mounted on its nose.*

○ *A device known as a Pitot tube may be used to determine the velocity of a fluid at a certain point.*

> **PRONUNCIATION**
>
> Note that you should not pronounce the "t" at the end of "Pitot" as it is a French word. /piːtoʊ/

piv|ot /pɪvət/ (**pivots**)

MACHINERY AND COMPONENTS

NOUN A **pivot** is a short shaft or pin supporting something that turns.

○ *The hands of a large clock are usually supported on pivots.*

○ *The turning effect of a lever depends on the force and its distance from the pivot.*

plane strain /pleɪn streɪn/

MECHANICS AND DYNAMICS

NOUN **Plane strain** is a two-dimensional state of strain in which all the shape changes of a material happen on a single plane.

○ Plane strain is applicable to forging, where deformation in a particular direction is constrained by the die wall.

○ The strain state is called plane strain when the deformation happens in a single plane.

plane stress /pleɪn strɛs/

MECHANICS AND DYNAMICS

NOUN **Plane stress** is a two-dimensional state of stress in which all stress is applied in a single plane.

○ Plane stress exists when one of the three principal stresses is zero.

○ In very flat or thin objects, the stresses are negligible in the smallest dimension so plane stress can be said to apply.

plas|tic de|for|ma|tion /plæstɪk dɪfɔrmeɪʃᵊn/

MATERIALS

NOUN In **plastic deformation** a material changes shape when a stress is applied to it and does not go back to its original state when the stress is removed.

○ Plastic deformation needs to occur in any metal forming operation.

○ Plastic deformation of a polycrystalline specimen corresponds to the comparable distortion of the individual grains by means of slip.

plate /pleɪt/ (**plates**)

GENERAL

NOUN A **plate** is a large flat piece of raw material, thicker than a sheet and thinner than a slab.

○ The final product is either metal sheet or plate, with the former being less than 0.24 inches thick and the latter greater than 0.24 inches.

○ The slabs are hot or cold rolled into sheet metal or plates.

pneu|mat|ic /numætɪk/

FLUID ENGINEERING

ADJECTIVE A **pneumatic** machine or device is operated by compressed air or by a vacuum.

○ A pneumatic drill uses compressed air to drive the drill bit into concrete.

○ The gas in pneumatic systems absorbs excessive force.

Pois|son's ra|ti|o /pwasoʊnz reɪʃoʊ/

MATERIALS

NOUN The **Poisson's ratio** is the decrease in the breadth or thickness of a bar when it is stretched by a particular amount. This term is named for French mathematician Siméon Poisson (1781–1840).

○ The ratio of the lateral contraction of a material to the longitudinal extension is Poisson's ratio.

○ Cork and concrete are materials with a very low value of Poisson's ratio.

pol|y|mer /pɒlɪmər/ (polymers)

MATERIALS

NOUN A **polymer** is a type of organic solid (= a solid that is a compound of carbon or hydrogen) that has a very large molecular structure.

○ A polymer is a substance composed of long chains of simpler units called monomers.

○ The major structural feature of polymers is the presence of a large number of monomeric units which are repeated many times.

pol|y|mer ma|trix com|po|site (ABBR **PMC**) /pɒlɪmər meɪtrɪks kəmpɑzɪt/ (polymer matrix composites)

MATERIALS

NOUN A **polymer matrix composite** is a material consisting of a composite made stronger by adding fibers or particles to it.

○ They used a polymer matrix composite, epoxy resin reinforced with glass fibers.

○ *Polymer matrix composites with continuous carbon fibers are used for aerospace, automobile, and civil structures.*

---

pop|pet /pɒpɪt/ (poppets)

FLUID ENGINEERING

NOUN A **poppet** is a mushroom-shaped valve often used as an exhaust or inlet valve in an internal-combustion engine.

○ *Poppets are sometimes called mushroom valves, because of their shape.*

○ *Poppet valves are used in most piston engines to open and close the exhaust ports in the cylinder heads.*

---

po|ros|i|ty /pɔrɒsɪti/

MANUFACTURING AND ASSEMBLY

NOUN The **porosity** of a solid is the existence of small empty spaces in it.

○ *Moisture inside the mold evaporated during the casting and the resulting metal had an unacceptable level of porosity.*

○ *As moisture transport is closely related to the formation of pores, the more water lost during cooling, the higher the porosity achieved.*

---

port /pɔrt/ (ports)

FLUID ENGINEERING

NOUN A **port** is an opening, usually controlled by a valve, by which fluid enters or leaves the cylinder head of a fluid machine.

○ *The exhaust process in a two stroke engine begins as soon as the exhaust port is uncovered by the piston during its downward motion.*

○ *The inlet port is the opening in the cylinder wall through which the charge is drawn in.*

▶ **COLLOCATIONS:**
exhaust port
inlet port
outlet port

P

Port|land ce|ment /ˈpɔːtlənd sɪmɛnt/

MECHANICS AND DYNAMICS

NOUN **Portland cement** is the type of cement usually used in buildings and bridges. Portland cement is so named because of its similarity to Portland stone, which was quarried on the Isle of Portland in Dorset, England.

○ Usually, the cementing material is Portland cement.

○ Cements using more than 60% slag as an aggregate are more resistant to sea water than pure Portland cement.

po|ten|tial flow /pəˈtɛnʃəl fləʊ/

FLUID ENGINEERING

NOUN **Potential flow** is a way of describing flow in a fluid using streamlines.

○ In a potential flow model, drift forces are due to a structure's ability to create waves.

○ The only requirement for potential flow is that the flow is irrotational.

pow|er /ˈpaʊər/

ENERGY, THERMODYNAMICS AND HEAT TRANSFER

NOUN **Power** is the rate at which energy is produced or used.

○ The watt is a unit of power, equal to one joule per second.

○ Power is usually transmitted through overhead cables.

press /prɛs/ (**presses**)

MANUFACTURING AND ASSEMBLY

NOUN A **press** is a machine that uses pressure to do a particular kind of work, for example to shape materials or extract liquids.

○ This type of forging involves squeezing metal between dies in a press.

○ The finely ground material is then placed in a filter cloth and the juice extracted in a press.

pres|sure ves|sel /prɛʃər vɛsəl/ (**pressure vessels**)

GENERAL

NOUN A **pressure vessel** is a container holding a fluid whose internal pressure is significantly higher than outside.

○ Because hydrogen must be intensely pressurized to several hundred atmospheres it must be stored in a pressure vessel.

○ Simply fill a pressure vessel with hot water at a high pressure, and open a valve leading to a suitable nozzle.

pro|jec|tile /prədʒɛktəl/ (**projectiles**)

MECHANICS AND DYNAMICS

NOUN A **projectile** is a body which is launched into the air and receives no further propulsion.

○ A bullet is a projectile propelled by a gun.

○ Feet per second is the unit of measurement used to express the speed of a projectile.

pro|por|tion|al /prəpɔrʃənəl/

CONTROL, INSTRUMENTATION AND METROLOGY

ADJECTIVE A **proportional** control is a type of control where the strength of the output is adjusted according to the difference between the current measure and the setpoint.

○ In this control system, the control effort is proportional to the error; the greater the error, the greater the effort.

○ A proportional controller continually adjusts the manipulated variable.

prox|im|i|ty probe /prɒksɪmɪti proʊb/ (**proximity probes**)

CONTROL, INSTRUMENTATION AND METROLOGY

NOUN A **proximity probe** is an instrument for measuring how far the surface of a component is away from the end of the probe.

○ A proximity probe is able to detect the presence of nearby objects without touching them.

○ *Shaft vibrations are measured with a pair of proximity probes mounted in the bearing housing close to the journal bearing.*

---

psy|chro|me|try /saɪkrɒmɪtri/

ENERGY, THERMODYNAMICS AND HEAT TRANSFER

NOUN **Psychrometry** is the study of the thermodynamics of gas-vapor mixtures.

○ *Psychrometry is the study of the properties of moist air and is useful to engineers concerned with heating, cooling, and ventilating buildings.*

○ *Psychrometry is the subject which deals with the properties of gas-vapor mixtures.*

---

pul|tru|sion /pʊltruʒ³n/

MANUFACTURING AND ASSEMBLY

NOUN **Pultrusion** is a process for making composite materials in which fibers and resin are pulled through a heated die.

○ *In some cases the composite is pulled through a very long die, in a process called pultrusion.*

○ *In pultrusion, resin-soaked reinforcements are pulled through a heated die where the resin is cured.*

---

pump /pʌmp/ (pumps)

FLUID ENGINEERING

NOUN A **pump** is a device used for moving a liquid.

○ *A pump forces the washer fluid to the nozzles.*

○ *A pump is a device for moving a liquid.*

Qq

qual|i|ty as|sur|ance (ABBR **QA**) /kwɒlɪti əʃʊərəns/

MANUFACTURING AND ASSEMBLY

NOUN **Quality assurance** involves making sure that no defective products are made during the manufacturing process.

- A mockup is often required for quality assurance, to ensure that architectural requirements and industry tolerances are met.

- Quality assurance is the process of making certain that products meet customers' expectations.

---

qual|i|ty sys|tem /kwɒlɪti sɪstəm/ (**quality systems**)

MANUFACTURING AND ASSEMBLY

NOUN A **quality system** is a structure for managing the quality of the output of a manufacturer.

- We have a very stringent quality system for inspecting items and delivering the best products.

- A good quality system prevents errors from occurring rather than correcting them after they have happened.

Rr

rack-and-pin|ion /ræk ənd pɪnyən/ (rack-and-pinions)

MACHINERY AND COMPONENTS

NOUN A **rack-and-pinion** is a device for changing rotary motion into linear motion, in which a gearwheel (the pinion) engages with a flat toothed bar (the rack).

○ On a rack-and-pinion steering system, the end of the steering shaft has a pinion gear that meshes with the rack.

○ A rack-and-pinion gear system prevents a train from slipping backward when going up a steep hill.

ra|di|a|tion /reɪdieɪʃ°n/

ENERGY, THERMODYNAMICS AND HEAT TRANSFER

NOUN **Radiation** is the flow of heat from one surface to another by infrared waves.

○ Solar cells generate electric power from the sun's radiation.

○ When two solid surfaces at different temperatures are separated by a transparent fluid phase, they will exchange thermal energy by radiation.

rake an|gle /reɪk æŋg°l/ (rake angles)

MANUFACTURING AND ASSEMBLY

NOUN The **rake angle** is the angle of the surface of a cutting tool tip over which the removed chips flow.

○ The rake angle is the angle between the front or cutting face of the tool and a line perpendicular to the workpiece.

○ If the rake angle is too small (say less than 10 degrees), it makes the cutting edge so thin that it may break under the strain of the work.

RELATED WORDS

Compare **rake angle** with **relief angle**, which is the angle between a cutting tool and the workpiece it has just cut.

---

ram /ræm/ (**rams**)

MACHINERY AND COMPONENTS

NOUN A **ram** is a piston or moving plate, especially one driven by hydraulic or pneumatic power.

○ A hydraulic ram drives the chisel into the material to be cut.

○ The pneumatic ram moves the rivet forward and rotates to place the rivet in alignment with the nose piece of the riveting tool.

---

ran|dom vi|bra|tion /rændəm vaɪbreɪʃⁿn/

MECHANICS AND DYNAMICS

NOUN **Random vibration** is a type of forced vibration in which the motion follows no regular pattern.

○ Random vibration is the kind of vibration experienced by a car driving along a bumpy road.

○ Random vibration is vibration whose amplitude is unpredictable.

Ran|kine cy|cle /ræŋkɪn saɪkᵊl/

ENERGY, THERMODYNAMICS AND HEAT TRANSFER

NOUN The **Rankine cycle** is a thermodynamic cycle in which power is produced from a liquid heated to produce steam. This term is named for Scottish engineer William Rankine (1820–1872).

○ The simplest vapor-power cycle is the Rankine cycle.

○ The Rankine cycle is also sometimes called the standard vapor power cycle.

r

---

rap|id pro|to|ty|ping /ræpɪd proʊtətaɪpɪŋ/

MANUFACTURING AND ASSEMBLY

NOUN **Rapid prototyping** is a process for producing solid objects in slices directly from a computer file.

○ Rapid prototyping is the technology used to make physical objects directly from CAD data sources.

○ The first techniques for rapid prototyping became available in the late 1980s and were used to produce models and prototype parts.

---

ratch|et /rætʃɪt/ (ratchets)

MACHINERY AND COMPONENTS

NOUN A **ratchet** is a device in which a rack or wheel with teeth is engaged by a pawl to allow motion in only one direction.

○ The pawl engages with the ratchet teeth to stop movement in a particular direction.

○ Operating as a ratchet, the clutch transmits torque in only one direction, free-wheeling in the other.

---

ream|ing /rɪ̱mɪŋ/

MANUFACTURING AND ASSEMBLY

NOUN **Reaming** is a cutting process in which a cutting tool produces a hole of a very accurate size.

○ Reaming is done to a hole which has been already drilled, to produce a truly circular hole of exactly the right diameter.

○ Reaming involves widening the opening of a hole.

---

re|frig|er|ant /rɪfrɪ̱dʒərənt/ (refrigerants)

ENERGY, THERMODYNAMICS AND HEAT TRANSFER

NOUN A **refrigerant** is a material whose boiling and condensation moves heat from one heat exchanger to another.

○ The three main refrigerants used in industrial refrigeration systems are light hydrocarbons such as propane, anhydrous ammonia, and chlorofluorocarbons.

○ Any substance which can be used to abstract heat from other substances, and thereby lower their temperatures, can be used as a refrigerant.

re|frig|er|a|tion /rɪfrɪdʒəreɪʃ°n/

ENERGY, THERMODYNAMICS AND HEAT TRANSFER

NOUN **Refrigeration** involves the boiling and condensation of a refrigerant to cool a surface or volume.

○ Refrigeration is a process which cools a closed space by removing heat from it.

○ A compressor is a component of a refrigeration system that pumps refrigerant and increases the pressure of the refrigerant vapor.

reg|is|ter /rɛdʒɪstər/ (registers, registered, registering)

MANUFACTURING AND ASSEMBLY

VERB If a mechanical part **registers**, it lines up with another.

○ When the tube is turned so that its hole registers with a second tube, fluid can flow from one tube to the other.

○ A port in the journal registers with a similar port in the bearing.

▶ COLLOCATION:
register with

reg|u|late /rɛgyəleɪt/ (regulates, regulated, regulating)

CONTROL, INSTRUMENTATION AND METROLOGY

VERB If you **regulate** an instrument or appliance, you adjust it so that it operates correctly.

○ A 3-speed fan means you can regulate the speed at which vapor is distributed.

○ By adjusting the thermostat, you can regulate the temperature of a building.

reg|u|la|tor /rɛgyəleɪtər/ (regulators)

CONTROL, INSTRUMENTATION AND METROLOGY

NOUN A **regulator** is a mechanism or device that controls something such as pressure, temperature, or fluid flow.

○ The voltage regulator keeps the power level stabilized.

○ The pressure regulator momentarily reduces the pressure in the brake lines to give the wheels a chance to keep spinning rather than locking up.

re|lay /ˈriːleɪ/ (relays)

CONTROL, INSTRUMENTATION AND METROLOGY

NOUN A **relay** is a device that controls the setting of a valve or switch automatically by means of an electric motor, solenoid, or pneumatic mechanism.

○ If the alarm is triggered, the relay automatically cuts off the heater.

○ When the relays are in the position shown, current will flow vertically upwards through the field coil.

re|lief an|gle /ˈriːliːf ˈæŋɡəl/ (relief angles)

MANUFACTURING AND ASSEMBLY

NOUN The **relief angle** is the angle between a cutting tool and the workpiece it has just cut.

○ The relief angle on a machine tool is the angle that the edge of the tool nearest the workpiece makes with the workpiece.

○ If the relief angle is too small the side of the tool will not clear the work and will rub.

re|lieved /rɪˈliːvd/

MANUFACTURING AND ASSEMBLY

ADJECTIVE A **relieved** component has part of its surface cut away to avoid friction or wear.

○ The rear part of the stock is relieved so that the bolt will not hit it during functioning.

○ Broad pieces of wood are frequently given a relieved back, a hidden groove or grooves that reduce the effective thickness of the piece and thus the tendency of the piece to cup.

re|new|a|ble en|er|gy /rɪˈnjuːəbəl ˈɛnərdʒi/

ENERGY, THERMODYNAMICS AND HEAT TRANSFER

NOUN **Renewable energy** is energy produced by wind, sun, and other sources that will never run out.

○ The cost of solar, wind, and other forms of renewable energy is getting cheaper.

○ Clean renewable energy is critical if we are to tackle global warming.

TYPES OF RENEWABLE ENERGY INCLUDE:

biofuel, geothermal power, hydropower, solar power, wind energy

---

re|vers|i|ble /rɪvɜrsɪbəl/

ENERGY, THERMODYNAMICS AND HEAT TRANSFER

ADJECTIVE A **reversible** thermodynamic process can happen in the reverse direction without changing the surroundings.

○ A typical example of a reversible thermodynamic process is when a gas expands without losing heat.

○ Although reversible heat transfer never occurs in nature, it is a useful construct in thermodynamics.

---

rhe|ol|o|gy /riɒlədʒi/

FLUID ENGINEERING

NOUN **Rheology** is the study of the flow of liquids which do not flow easily.

○ Rheology studies the flow of unusual materials, particularly non-Newtonian fluids.

○ Rheology is the study of the flow of any material under the influence of an applied force or stress.

---

rig|id bod|y /rɪdʒɪd bɒdi/ (**rigid bodies**)

MECHANICS AND DYNAMICS

NOUN A **rigid body** is a body that does not deform or vibrate.

○ Continuum mechanics deals with deformable bodies, as opposed to rigid bodies.

○ A rigid body is one where every atom is always in the same position with respect to every other atom in the body, even when outside forces are applied to the body.

ris|er /ˈraɪzər/ (**risers**)

MANUFACTURING AND ASSEMBLY

NOUN A **riser** is a pipe or duct up which a fluid flows.

○ Oil travels up through the riser to the surface.

○ Molten metal is poured into the casting through a runner, displacing air which escapes through a riser.

ro|bot /ˈroʊbət/ (**robots**)

CONTROL, INSTRUMENTATION AND METROLOGY

NOUN A **robot** is a mechanical device with a control system that makes it able to carry out tasks automatically.

○ Robots have replaced humans in doing many repetitive and dangerous tasks.

○ Robots are used extensively in industrial engineering because they allow businesses to save money on labor.

ro|bot arm /ˈroʊbət ɑrm/ (**robot arms**)

MANUFACTURING AND ASSEMBLY

NOUN A **robot arm** is a type of robot consisting of parts linked together in the same way as those of a human arm, mounted on a stand.

○ The most common manufacturing robot is the robot arm which is usually made up of several metal segments.

○ Sensors were fixed to the robot arm to detect whether there were humans close to the robot.

rock|er /ˈrɒkər/ (**rockers**)

MACHINERY AND COMPONENTS

NOUN A **rocker** is a device that operates with a rocking motion.

○ A rocker switch breaks and connects the electrical circuit by "rocking" in one direction to break the circuit, and in the other direction to connect the circuit.

○ As the rocker arm rocks up, it pushes the valve down in the opposite direction.

rod /rɒd/ (rods)

GENERAL

NOUN A **rod** is a long circular bar of raw material.

○ A dipstick is a metal rod with marks along one end, used to measure the amount of liquid in a container.

○ The connecting rod connects the piston to the crank or crankshaft.

roll|er bear|ing /roʊlər bɛərɪŋ/ (roller bearings)

MACHINERY AND COMPONENTS

NOUN A **roller bearing** is a bearing in which a shaft runs on steel rollers held in a cage.

○ Friction is reduced in car wheels using roller bearings.

○ Roller bearings typically have higher radial load capacity than ball bearings.

roll|ing bear|ing /roʊlɪŋ bɛərɪŋ/ (rolling bearings)

MACHINERY AND COMPONENTS

NOUN A **rolling bearing** is a bearing in which friction is reduced by the rolling action of balls or rollers.

○ Ball bearings and roller bearings are both examples of rolling bearings.

○ There are five types of rolling-elements that are used in rolling bearings: balls, cylindrical rollers, tapered rollers, spherical rollers, and needles.

roll|ing re|sist|ance /roʊlɪŋ rɪzɪstəns/

GENERAL

NOUN The **rolling resistance** of a wheel or ball is its resistance to movement caused by friction between it and the surface it is rolling on.

○ The rolling resistance of the tires is a major opposing force on a moving vehicle.

○ The extremely narrow front wheels of a drag-race car are used to reduce rolling resistance.

ro|ta|tion /roʊteɪʃ°n/

MECHANICS AND DYNAMICS

NOUN **Rotation** is the movement of a body around a center.

○ Rotation of the propeller in one direction will drive the boat forward and in the opposite direction will drive it backward.

○ The complete engine cycle occupies one rotation of the crank and two piston strokes.

run|ner /rʌnər/ (**runners**)

MANUFACTURING AND ASSEMBLY

NOUN A **runner** is a channel through which molten material flows into a casting mold.

○ During casting, molten metal flows along runners to different points in the mold cavity.

○ Molten metal is poured into the casting through a runner, displacing air which escapes through a riser.

R

Ss

---

safe|ty valve /seɪfti vælv/ (safety valves)

GENERAL

NOUN A **safety valve** is a valve in a pressure vessel that lets fluid escape when the pressure becomes too high.

○ When the steam pressure reaches 15 psi the safety valve opens and excess steam escapes.

○ A safety valve is a valve that opens to release excess pressure or heat.

---

sand cast|ing /sænd kæstɪŋ/

MANUFACTURING AND ASSEMBLY

NOUN **Sand casting** is a process in which a molten metal is poured into a mold made from sand.

○ Metal castings can be produced in sand molds. This is sand casting.

○ Shell molding is similar to sand casting, but the molding cavity is formed by a hardened "shell" of sand instead of a flask filled with sand.

---

screw¹ /skru/ (screws)

MACHINERY AND COMPONENTS

NOUN A **screw** is a metal device for fastening materials together. It consists of a shank with sharp threads that cut their own thread in a material as the screw is rotated with a screwdriver.

○ Remove the screws with a screwdriver.

○ Tighten all screws gradually, in rotation.

S

screw² /skru/ (screws, screwed, screwing)

MANUFACTURING AND ASSEMBLY

VERB If you **screw** a screw or bolt, you rotate it to put it into or take it out of a material.

○ Screw the screws tightly.

○ The cap can be screwed in using a small screwdriver.

▶ COLLOCATION:
screw in

seal /sil/ (seals)

MACHINERY AND COMPONENTS

NOUN A **seal** is a part fitted around or between other parts of a machine to prevent fluid from leaking in or out.

○ The seal around the edge of the door had split and water had got in.

○ The connection has a watertight seal to prevent water entering the chamber.

self-tap|ping /sɛlf tæpɪŋ/

MACHINERY AND COMPONENTS

ADJECTIVE A **self-tapping** screw cuts its own thread when it is screwed into a plain hole in a metal sheet.

○ Self-tapping screws are hardened so that their threads cut mating threads in one or both of the steel parts being connected.

○ Self-tapping screws that create their own threads are widely used with all thermoplastic parts.

sen|sor /sɛnsər/ (sensors)

CONTROL, INSTRUMENTATION AND METROLOGY

NOUN A **sensor** is an instrument for detecting a quantity or quality, for example temperature or motion, and returning an electrical output.

○ The gun has a sensor that gauges the distance a person is away from it.

○ Strain can be measured by fiber-optic sensors embedded in the composite.

set|point /sɛtpɔɪnt/ (**setpoints**)

CONTROL, INSTRUMENTATION AND METROLOGY

NOUN A **setpoint** is a state that a control system is aiming to reach.

- ○ *The temperature setpoint of a heating system is the temperature the control system aims to reach.*
- ○ *A setpoint is determined, usually by the user, and the valve is adjusted so that flow reaches that point.*

shaft /ʃæft/ (**shafts**)

GENERAL

NOUN A **shaft** is a revolving rod that transmits motion or power.

- ○ *The crankshaft transmits the vertical motion of the pistons to a rotational motion of the gearbox input shaft.*
- ○ *A propeller shaft for a small yacht is made of a solid steel bar 100mm in diameter.*

shaft en|cod|er /ʃæft ɪnkoʊdər/ (**shaft encoders**)

CONTROL, INSTRUMENTATION AND METROLOGY

NOUN A **shaft encoder** is a sensor for measuring how fast a shaft rotates.

- ○ *The rotation rate of the car engine is measured by a shaft encoder.*
- ○ *A shaft encoder is an electro-mechanical device that converts the angular position of a shaft or axle to an analog or digital code.*

shear /ʃɪər/

MECHANICS AND DYNAMICS

NOUN **Shear** is the movement of one surface of a substance over another parallel surface.

- ○ *Viscosity is related to the rate of shear in a fluid.*
- ○ *Longitudinal shear is a movement of one joint face in a direction parallel to the longitudinal axis of the joint.*

shear force /ʃɪər fɔrs/

MECHANICS AND DYNAMICS

NOUN **Shear force** is force that makes one surface of a substance move over another parallel surface.

○ The car engine mountings are subject to a shear force from the weight of the engine.

○ Tensile and compressive force acts perpendicular to a structure's surface whereas shear force acts parallel to the surface.

shear mod|u|lus /ʃɪər mɒdʒələs/

MATERIALS

NOUN The **shear modulus** of a material is how stiff or rigid it is. It is equal to the shear stress divided by the shear strain.

○ The shear modulus is defined as the ratio of shear stress to shear strain.

○ The shear modulus characterizes how difficult it is to distort a substance's shape by shear stress.

shear stress /ʃɪər strɛs/

MECHANICS AND DYNAMICS

NOUN **Shear stress** is shear force divided by the area of the surface on which it is acting.

○ To calculate the shear stress of a material you need to know the shear force and the area of the material.

○ A force applied to an area of a liquid confined between two plates, sufficient to set the liquid in motion, is known as shear stress.

sheet /ʃit/ (**sheets**)

GENERAL

NOUN A **sheet** of raw material is a large, flat, thin piece, usually up to a few millimeters thick.

○ Most mirrors are made from a sheet of metal with glass on the front to protect it.

○ A steel strip is a sheet of steel less than 600 mm wide.

shell /ʃɛl/ (shells)

GENERAL

NOUN The **shell** of a machine or vehicle is its basic structure.

○ *The car's shell (minus the doors, trunk lid, hood, and fenders) is lowered onto the chassis so the bodywork can be assembled.*

○ *Editing techniques let designers create shells of products such as fuselages.*

shield|ed met|al arc weld|ing (ABBR **SMAW**) /ʃildɪd mɛtᵊl ɑrk weldɪŋ/

MANUFACTURING AND ASSEMBLY

NOUN **Shielded metal arc welding** is a process in which a coated wire is melted to fill spaces between parts. The molten coating floats to the surface of the molten metal to protect it from the atmosphere.

○ *Shielded metal arc welding is also called stick welding and it uses the simplest equipment of any arc welding process.*

○ *In shielded metal arc welding, an electrical circuit is established between the workpiece and the welding electrode.*

shim /ʃɪm/ (shims)

MANUFACTURING AND ASSEMBLY

NOUN A **shim** is a small object or piece of material used, for example, to create a little extra height or a little extra space.

○ *You may need some shims to get the surface of the square plate up above the surface of the thrust plate.*

○ *A shim is a thin flat hard metal strip produced to close tolerances.*

S

shock wave /ʃɒk weɪv/ (**shock waves**)

NOUN A **shock wave** is a type of wave in a fluid in which there is a sudden change in pressure, for example when a very fast solid object moves in the fluid.

○ The energy of the blast caused a shock wave to travel through the water.

○ Pressurized gas is released into a shock tube to generate a shock wave.

shoul|der /ʃoʊldər/ (**shoulders**)

NOUN A **shoulder** is a large projection or a part of something where the shape or diameter changes suddenly, designed to withstand thrust.

○ The retaining rings create a rigid shoulder which can retain thrust loads.

○ These bearings have an extended shoulder on one end of the outer ring, allowing angular contact between the shaft and bearing during times of high thrust.

shrink|age /ʃrɪŋkɪdʒ/

NOUN **Shrinkage** is a reduction in the volume of a material.

○ Shrinkage occurs when molten metal solidifies because metals are less dense as a liquid than as a solid.

○ Shrinkage is the reduction of the dimensions of a plastic part, compared with its mold dimensions.

shut-off /ʃʌt ɔf/ (**shut-offs**)

NOUN A **shut-off** is a device that turns something off, especially a machine control.

○ Most gasoline pumps have an automatic shut-off that turns off the pump when the car's gas tank is nearly full.

○ If the airflow fails, the temperature of the heater rises suddenly, and the control system can execute an immediate shut-off.

slab /slæb/ (slabs)

GENERAL

NOUN A **slab** is a large, flat, thick piece of raw material, usually a few inches thick.

○ *Sidewalks are usually made from concrete slabs.*

○ *Horizontal slabs of steel reinforced concrete, usually between 100 and 500mm thick, are used to build floors and ceilings.*

slag /slæg/

MANUFACTURING AND ASSEMBLY

NOUN **Slag** is a molten oxide that floats on the surface of a molten metal and protects it.

○ *The melted metal may be covered with a protecting slag.*

○ *Slag is a product resulting from the action of a flux on the non-metallic constituents of a processed ore.*

slave /sleɪv/ (slaves)

GENERAL

NOUN A **slave** is a device that is controlled by another similar device or that copies the action of another similar device.

○ *Most hydraulic braking systems have one master cylinder near the pedal with slave cylinders on each wheel.*

○ *The pins that retain the slave (or link) rods in the master rod are called link pins.*

sleeve /sliv/ (sleeves)

MACHINERY AND COMPONENTS

NOUN A **sleeve** is a tube of material that is put into a cylindrical bore, for example to reduce the diameter of the bore or to line it with a different material.

○ *Sometimes there is a metal sleeve in the bore to give it more strength.*

○ *The pistons run directly in the bores without using cast iron sleeves.*

S

slide valve /slaɪd vælv/ (**slide valves**)

FLUID ENGINEERING

NOUN A **slide valve** is a valve that slides across a hole to open and close it.

○ When the slide valve slides to one side, it uncovers the intake port and allows steam to fill the cylinder.

○ In the power industry, large size slide valves are used in main steam and feed lines to isolate sections of the plant.

slug flow /slʌg floʊ/

FLUID ENGINEERING

NOUN **Slug flow** exists in a fluid when large bubbles of gas form in it making lumps of particles move.

○ As gas velocity is increased, large bubbles rise through the bed, carrying above them aggregates of solid particles. This phenomenon is known as slug flow.

○ The invention separates the liquid and gas phases of a liquid/gas mixture and eliminates slug flow.

sock|et /sɒkɪt/ (**sockets**)

GENERAL

NOUN A **socket** is a part with an opening or hollow into which some other part can be fitted.

○ The lower end of the bracket fits into a socket in the bracket support.

○ If you overtighten these screws, you can pop the ball right out of its socket.

sol|id mod|el /sɒlɪd mɒdəl/ (**solid models**)

MANUFACTURING AND ASSEMBLY

NOUN A **solid model** is a representation of a solid (= not liquid or gas) object produced by a computer and used in simulation.

○ Students use the computer and CAD system to create 3-D solid models of various machine components.

○ The software helps the designer create solid models of virtually every type of cam.

spin|dle /spɪnd³l/ (spindles)

GENERAL

NOUN A **spindle** is a rod, especially one that rotates and acts as an axle, mandrel, or arbor.

○ The workpiece rotates on a spindle called an arbor.

○ The cutting tool can be mounted on or in the spindle of a machine tool.

spline /splaɪn/ (splines)

GENERAL

NOUN **Splines** are narrow ridges around the circumference of a shaft (external splines) or the grooves that these ridges fit into (internal splines). They are used to prevent rotational movement between two parts.

○ The lower part has four external splines that mate with four internal ones in the upper part.

○ Splines are straight slots machined along a shaft so that a hole similarly machined on its inside can slide freely on the shaft.

spot weld /spɒt wɛld/ (spot welds)

MANUFACTURING AND ASSEMBLY

NOUN A **spot weld** is a join that has been spot-welded.

○ Spot welds are made by pressing electrodes against both sides of the metal parts to be joined and passing a high current through them.

○ Spot welds are mainly used for joining parts which will be stressed in such as way that the welds are in shear.

spot-weld /spɒt wɛld/ (spot-welds, spot-welded, spot-welding)

MANUFACTURING AND ASSEMBLY

VERB If two pieces of metal, especially wires or sheets, are **spot-welded**, they are joined by melting small circular areas on the metal using heat from an electric current and pressure.

S

○ The metal sheets are spot-welded by concentrating an electric current on a small spot, melting the metal there and forming a weld.

○ On ice-skates, the steel blade is spot-welded to the tubular frame.

---

spring /sprɪŋ/ (springs)

GENERAL

NOUN A **spring** is a device, such as a coil or strip of steel, that stores potential energy when it is compressed, stretched, or bent and releases it when the restraining force is removed.

○ As a spring is compressed or stretched, the force it applies changes.

○ The solenoid, being spring-loaded, snapped back into place.

---

sprock|et /sprɒkɪt/ (sprockets)

MACHINERY AND COMPONENTS

NOUN A **sprocket** is a fairly thin wheel with teeth projecting outwards from the rim, especially a wheel that drives or is driven by a chain.

○ When you ride a bicycle, the teeth of the sprocket mesh with the chain.

○ The chain makes a continuous circuit between the driven rear-wheel sprocket and the smaller, driving front one.

---

spur gear /spɜr gɪər/ (spur gears)

MACHINERY AND COMPONENTS

NOUN A **spur gear** is a gear with teeth that project outwards from a cylindrical surface. Two spur gears are used to transmit power between parallel shafts.

○ In spur gears, the edge of each tooth is parallel to the axis of rotation and they mesh together when they are fitted to parallel shafts.

○ Spur gears are the simplest form of gears.

---

sta|bil|i|ty /stəbɪlɪti/

CONTROL, INSTRUMENTATION AND METROLOGY

NOUN The **stability** of a control system is how easily it can be made to operate at a setpoint without fluctuating.

○ The stability of a nuclear reactor control system is very important because if it does not behave in a predictable way, there could be a nuclear accident.

○ Control is needed to improve the stability of a process.

---

stain|less steel /ˈsteɪnlɪs stil/

MATERIALS

NOUN **Stainless steel** is a type of steel which has had chromium added to it. This improves its resistance to corrosion.

○ Stainless steel does not corrode or rust outdoors as ordinary steel does.

○ Stainless steel is used for making knives and forks, kitchen sinks, surgical instruments and automobile parts.

---

stat|ic head /ˈstætɪk hɛd/

FLUID ENGINEERING

NOUN **Static head** is the pressure resulting from a column of liquid acting under gravity.

○ The weight of a fluid in a container exerts pressure on the containing vessel's sides and bottom. This is called static head pressure and is caused by Earth's gravitational pull.

○ Static head can be raised by lifting the source point, lowering the pump inlet, or raising the level of fluid in the suction vessel.

---

stat|ics /ˈstætɪks/

MECHANICS AND DYNAMICS

NOUN **Statics** is the study of internal and external forces in a structure.

○ Statics is the branch of mechanics that deals with bodies at rest.

○ The study of systems in which momentum does not change is called statics, whereas dynamics involves the study of changes in momentum.

sta|tis|ti|cal pro|cess con|trol /stətɪstɪkᵊl prɒsɛs kəntroʊl/

NOUN **Statistical process control** is a method used for maintaining quality in a manufacturing process by measuring characteristics of a product and using deviations from the ideal to adjust the process.

○ *Employees were trained in statistical process control, a method of monitoring defects and setting goals to reduce them.*

○ *Statistical process control is a method of quality management that registers quality deviations.*

stead|y-state /stɛdi steɪt/

ADJECTIVE **Steady-state** heat or mass flow is even, and heat or mass does not gather in a particular area.

○ *Under conditions of steady-state conservative flow the throughput across the entrance to a pipe is equal to the throughput at the exit.*

○ *It is essential to maintain a constant top surface temperature, and hence maintain steady-state conditions, if a billet with a consistent microstructure is to be produced.*

▶ COLLOCATION:
steady-state flow

steam boil|er /stim bɔɪlər/ (**steam boilers**)

NOUN A **steam boiler** is a container in which water is heated to produce steam.

○ *The steam boiler has a longer on-off cycle because steam has to be produced each time there is a call for heat.*

○ *Steam turbines generally require high-pressure steam boilers, so you have the maintenance of the boiler system as well as their turbine to consider.*

steam tur|bine /stim tɜrbɪn/ (**steam turbines**)

ENERGY, THERMODYNAMICS AND HEAT TRANSFER

NOUN A **steam turbine** is a type of electric power generator in which a shaft is made to rotate by the movement of steam past sets of blades arranged in circles.

○ *Modern steam-powered systems burn coal or gas to generate steam in boilers, which is then run through a steam turbine.*

○ *Gas turbines can be started up very quickly from cold but steam turbines cannot because it takes a while to get the boilers up to temperature and pressure.*

steel /stil/

MATERIALS

NOUN **Steel** is any iron-based alloy containing less than 1.5 percent carbon.

○ *Steel, an alloy consisting mostly of iron and a small amount of carbon, is one of the most common materials in the world.*

○ *Any steel containing thirteen or more percent chromium is classified as stainless.*

ste|re|o|li|tho|gra|phy /stɛrioʊlɪθɒɡrəfi/

MANUFACTURING AND ASSEMBLY

NOUN **Stereolithography** is a process for making models and parts in which a solid is built up a layer at a time by hardening parts of a container of resin using light.

○ *In stereolithography, parts are produced by successive solidification of thin resin layers using a UV laser beam.*

○ *Stereolithography enables solid, plastic, three-dimensional models to be made from CAD drawings in a matter of hours.*

S

strain /streɪn/

MATERIALS

NOUN **Strain** is a measure of how much a material changes shape under a force. It is equal to the change in any dimension divided by the original value of that dimension.

○ Strain is a measure of the deformation of a body, for example the proportional increase in length when a wire is stretched.

○ The average linear strain is obtained by dividing the elongation of the length of the specimen by the original length.

RELATED WORDS

Compare **strain** with **stress**, which is a measure of the internal forces in a material that changes shape under a force. It is equal to the force acting on the material divided by the cross-sectional area over which it is acting.

---

strain gage or strain gauge /streɪn geɪdʒ/ (strain gages)

CONTROL, INSTRUMENTATION AND METROLOGY

NOUN A **strain gage** is a sensor for measuring the amount of strain on a solid surface.

○ The deformation of the gearbox was measured using strain gages mounted at various points on its surface.

○ Strain gages mounted on the bar measure axial and transverse strain.

stream|line /ˈstriːmlaɪn/ (streamlines)

FLUID ENGINEERING

NOUN A **streamline** is a line which shows the direction of a flow.

○ Fluid particles move in definite paths or streamlines, which can be observed by adding a special powder to the flow.

○ A streamline is a continuous line through a fluid so that it has the direction of the velocity vector at every point.

stress /strɛs/

MATERIALS

NOUN **Stress** is a measure of the internal forces in a material that changes shape under a force. It is equal to the force acting on the material divided by the cross-sectional area over which it is acting.

○ The largest stress that a rod of material can withstand is known as its ultimate tensile strength.

○ Process annealing is a process used to relieve stress in a cold-worked carbon steel.

stress con|cen|tra|tion /strɛs kɒnsəntreɪʃən/ (**stress concentrations**)

MECHANICS AND DYNAMICS

NOUN A **stress concentration** in a solid is a place where there is a lot of stress, either because a force is applied in a particular area or there is a change in the cross-sectional area.

○ Notches and variation in cross section throughout a part lead to stress concentrations where fatigue cracks start.

○ The material is susceptible to fracture at points of stress concentration.

stress cor|ro|sion crack|ing /strɛs kərouʒən krækɪŋ/

MATERIALS

NOUN **Stress corrosion cracking** is a type of corrosion that can happen when a stress is present, resulting in cracks in the surface of metal.

○ Stress corrosion cracking is the formation of cracks in a material through the simultaneous action of a tensile stress and a corrosive environment.

○ Stress corrosion cracking has become one of the main reasons for the failure of steam generator tubing.

stress re|lax|a|tion /strɛs rilækseɪʃən/

MECHANICS AND DYNAMICS

NOUN **Stress relaxation** is a gradual reduction in stress with time at constant strain.

○ *Stress relaxation occurs in polymers when they are held in a strained state for long periods of time.*

○ *These alloys have very good resistance to stress relaxation and are therefore used as spring materials.*

---

stress re|lief /strɛs rɪlif/

MANUFACTURING AND ASSEMBLY

NOUN **Stress relief** involves removing stresses in a material, usually by heating it to a temperature at which it can deform easily.

○ *One form of stress relief is heating a metal to a high enough temperature for creep to occur and the plastic flow to gradually relieve the stress in the casting.*

○ *Vibration can be used as a method of stress relief, but the only proven technique is the use of heat treatment at a high enough temperature for creep to occur.*

---

stud /stʌd/ (studs)

GENERAL

NOUN A **stud** is a bolt without a flat top part, that is threaded at both ends but not in the center.

○ *The studs are first screwed into the cylinder block and the cylinder head is put over the projecting ends.*

○ *After the nut has been tightened, make sure the bolt or stud has at least one thread showing past the nut.*

---

sump /sʌmp/ (sumps)

MACHINERY AND COMPONENTS

NOUN A **sump** is a container, such as the lower part of the crankcase of an internal-combustion engine, into which liquids can drain and be used again.

○ *The oil drains into the sump so there is no build-up in the crankcase.*

○ *An oil pump takes oil from the sump at the bottom of the crankcase and feeds it through pipes to the bearings of the crankshaft.*

su|per|heat|ing /suːpərhiːtɪŋ/

ENERGY, THERMODYNAMICS AND HEAT TRANSFER

NOUN **Superheating** of steam is raising its temperature to well above boiling point.

○ *The use of superheating prevents the steam condensing in the engine.*

○ *Superheating is critical for compressors because without it the compressor may be provided with a liquid gas mixture, which can destroy the gas compressor because liquid is uncompressible.*

> **WORD BUILDER**
> **super-** = extremely
>
> The prefix **super-** appears in several words meaning "extreme" or "extremely:" **superheating**, **supersonic**.

su|per|son|ic /suːpərsɒnɪk/

FLUID ENGINEERING

ADJECTIVE **Supersonic** is used to describe things that move faster than the speed of sound in a particular medium, usually the air.

○ *These aircraft tolerate any pilot demands from ridiculously low speeds to supersonic flight.*

○ *Most modern firearm bullets are supersonic, traveling faster than the speed of sound.*

sur|face treat|ment /sɜrfɪs triːtmənt/ (**surface treatments**)

MANUFACTURING AND ASSEMBLY

NOUN A **surface treatment** is a process applied to the surface of a material to make it better in some way, for example by making it more resistant to corrosion or wear.

○ *Shot peening is a surface treatment in which small hard pellets are shot against the surface of a metal to make it more resistant to fatigue.*

○ *Silver plating is a surface treatment that can be applied to a broad range of different metals.*

S

sys|tem /sɪstəm/ (**systems**)

ENERGY, THERMODYNAMICS AND HEAT TRANSFER

NOUN In thermodynamics, a **system** is an entity within which energy is conserved.

○ *The total energy of a thermodynamic system remains constant, even if it is converted from one form to another.*

○ *An isolated thermodynamic system is not influenced in any way by its surroundings.*

S

Tt

---

tap /tæp/ (taps, tapped, tapping)

VERB If you **tap** an object or material, you cut a female screw thread in it using a specially designed tool.

○ The tool can tap a thread right through a piece of steel to enable a bolt to be screwed into it.

○ If your block does not have two threaded mounting holes, then some will need to be drilled and tapped to accept the pipe.

▶ **COLLOCATIONS:**
tap a bore
tap a hole
tap a thread

---

tap|pet /tæpɪt/ (tappets)

NOUN A **tappet** is a part that transfers motion from one machine part to another, especially the part of an internal-combustion engine that transmits motion from the camshaft to the push rods or valves.

○ The cam pushes on the tappet, which is a part of the rod and thus the rod is pushed upward.

○ Without a tappet, the sideways force created by the rotating cam would cause the valve stem to bend.

---

tem|per|a|ture /tɛmprətʃər/ (temperatures)

NOUN The **temperature** of a substance is related to the amount of heat that has been absorbed by it.

t

○ The samples were exposed to temperatures of around 2000 degrees Fahrenheit.

○ Thermoplastic materials melt when heated to a certain temperature, but harden again as they cool.

> **TALKING ABOUT TEMPERATURE**
>
> If the temperature goes up, you can say it **increases** or **rises**.
>
> If the temperature goes down, you can say it **drops** or **falls**.

ten|sile strength /tɛnsɪl strɛŋkθ/

MATERIALS

NOUN The **tensile strength** of a material is the maximum stress that can be applied to it before it breaks.

○ The tensile strength of aluminum alloys can be increased by special treatments.

○ Because of their high tensile strength, these products are suitable for boring in drilling machines.

> **RELATED WORDS**
>
> Compare **tensile strength** with **fracture toughness**, which is how likely a material is to resist fracture.

ten|sile stress /tɛnsɪl strɛs/

MECHANICS AND DYNAMICS

NOUN **Tensile stress** is stress which stretches a body in a particular direction.

○ The properties of metals are normally measured under tensile stress.

○ Tensile stress is the stress state that causes materials to stretch.

ten|sion /tɛnʃ°n/

MECHANICS AND DYNAMICS

NOUN The **tension** of a string, cable, etc is how much it is being stretched.

○ *Adjust the tension to loosen or tighten the belt.*

○ *Turning a small screw increases or decreases the tension of the spring.*

---

ten|sor /tɛnsər/ (**tensors**)

MECHANICS AND DYNAMICS

NOUN A **tensor** is a quantity, for example a stress or a strain, which has magnitude, direction, and a plane in which it acts.

○ *Stress and strain are both tensor quantities.*

○ *In real engineering components, stress and strain are 3-D tensors.*

---

ther|mal stress /θɜrməl strɛs/

MECHANICS AND DYNAMICS

NOUN **Thermal stress** is stress caused by differences in temperature or by differences in thermal expansion.

○ *A crack formed as a result of thermal stress produced by rapid cooling from a high temperature.*

○ *Because the section of rail was fixed at both ends it experienced a thermal stress when the ambient temperature increased.*

---

ther|mo|cou|ple /θɜrməkʌpəl/ (**thermocouples**)

CONTROL, INSTRUMENTATION AND METROLOGY

NOUN A **thermocouple** is a device made from two metal wires, which is used to measure temperature.

○ *The temperature inside the furnace was measured using a thermocouple.*

○ *Thermocouples are temperature sensors formed from the junction of two wires with different compositions.*

WORD BUILDER
thermo- = related to temperature

The prefix **thermo-** is used in several words that relate to temperature: **thermodynamics**, **thermometer**, **thermoplastic**, **thermoset**.

ther|mo|dy|nam|ics /θɜrmoʊdaɪnæmɪks/

ENERGY, THERMODYNAMICS AND HEAT TRANSFER

NOUN **Thermodynamics** is the study of the transfer and conversion of energy.

○ Thermodynamics, the science dealing with energy and its transformation, underlies the design of all power stations.

○ At its simplest, thermodynamics is the study of energy, its use, and its transformation through a system.

ther|mom|e|ter /θərmɒmɪtər/ (**thermometers**)

CONTROL, INSTRUMENTATION AND METROLOGY

NOUN A **thermometer** is a device for measuring temperature, usually one that works by the expansion of a column of fluid.

○ Measure the temperature of the water with a digital thermometer.

○ Mercury is used in thermometers because it expands when it is heated.

ther|mo|plas|tic /θɜrmoʊplæstɪk/

MATERIALS

ADJECTIVE A **thermoplastic** polymer can be melted and solidified many times.

○ The advantage of thermoplastic polymers is that they can be melted and resolidified.

○ Thermoplastic materials can be melted again and again.

ther|mo|set /θɜrməsɛt/

MATERIALS

ADJECTIVE A **thermoset** polymer forms by the reaction of two or more components or by curing (= hardening).

○ Thermoset polymers assume a permanent shape or set when they are cured.

○ Widely used thermoset plastics include Epoxy, Polyester, Silicone, and Urethane.

thread /θrɛd/ (**threads**)

GENERAL

NOUN A **thread** is a helical-shaped groove cut in a cylindrical hole (the female thread), or a helical-shaped ridge on a cylindrical bar, rod, shank, etc (the male thread).

○ *A tap is used to cut the helical groove that fits the thread of the screw.*

○ *A threading die is used to cut threads on a pipe.*

throt|tle /θrɒtᵊl/ (**throttles**)

GENERAL

NOUN A **throttle** is a device that controls the quantity of fuel or fuel and air mixture entering an engine.

○ *When the throttle is opened more fuel and air is injected into the engine to be burned.*

○ *The throttle is a valve that directly regulates the amount of air entering the engine.*

thrust /θrʌst/

MECHANICS AND DYNAMICS

NOUN **Thrust** is pressure that is exerted continuously by one object against another, especially the axial force by or on a shaft.

○ *An airplane generates thrust when air is pushed in the direction opposite to flight.*

○ *Thrust is generated along the shaft axis in helical gears, which has to be counteracted with special bearings.*

thrust bear|ing /θrʌst bɛərɪŋ/ (**thrust bearings**)

MACHINERY AND COMPONENTS

NOUN A **thrust bearing** is a type of bearing that helps rotation and resists thrust at the same time.

○ *The main function of a thrust bearing is to resist any axial force applied to the rotor and maintain its position.*

○ *Because helical gears have angular teeth, their operation produces axial thrusts that must be absorbed by thrust bearings.*

t

tol|er|ance /tɒlərəns/ (tolerances)

MANUFACTURING AND ASSEMBLY

NOUN A **tolerance** is the amount of variation that is allowed in a measurement or other characteristic of an object or workpiece.

○ The thermocouple has a tolerance of plus or minus 2.5 degrees at 1000 degrees C.

○ Because it had to fit neatly into the bearing, the shaft had to be machined to a tight tolerance.

tool /tul/ (tools)

GENERAL

NOUN A **tool** is a device, usually a simple one, for making or assembling components or parts.

○ A wrench is a tool for turning nuts or bolts.

○ Equipment such as axes, pry bars, saws, hammers, and shovels, are considered hand tools.

tool|ing /tulɪŋ/

GENERAL

NOUN **Tooling** consists of a set of tools used to manufacture a particular component, part, or assembly.

○ The company manufactures specialized tooling, including step drills and made-to-print cutters.

○ Expensive tooling will produce the items faster and will last longer.

tooth /tuθ/ (teeth)

GENERAL

NOUN The **teeth** on a gear, sprocket, or rack are the parts that stick out from it and mate with teeth on another part to transmit motion.

○ As the gear teeth mesh, they roll and slide over each other.

○ The crankshaft gear has 34 teeth.

torque /tɔrk/

MECHANICS AND DYNAMICS

NOUN **Torque** is the ability of a shaft to cause rotation.

○ You generate torque when you apply a force using a wrench.

○ A handle allows a user to apply torque to the central pendulum to start the system.

> **PRONUNCIATION**
>
> Note that **torque** only has one syllable. It comes from the Latin *torquere*, which means "to twist."

tor|sion /tɔrʃᵊn/

MECHANICS AND DYNAMICS

NOUN **Torsion** is the twisting of a part by applying equal and opposite torques at either end.

○ Ways to put an item into torsion include holding one end of it still while you twist the other end, or twisting both ends in opposite directions.

○ A shaft in torsion is sometimes used as a spring, for example in self-closing screen doors.

tran|si|ent /trænʃənt/

ENERGY, THERMODYNAMICS AND HEAT TRANSFER

ADJECTIVE A **transient** state changes with time.

○ This is known as a transient phase because it usually lasts less than a second.

○ Since the event is transient, it is difficult to locate the particle and study it.

trans|mit /trænzmɪt/ (**transmits, transmitted, transmitting**)

GENERAL

VERB To **transmit** something such as a force, motion, or power means to transfer it from one part of a mechanical system to another.

○ A spinning shaft transmits power from the clutch to the gearbox.

○ Conductance is the ability of a material to transmit an electrical charge.

t

▶ **COLLOCATIONS:**
transmit a force
transmit a movement
transmit an impulse
transmit energy
transmit power

---

tri|bol|o|gy /traɪbɒlədʒi/

MATERIALS

NOUN **Tribology** is the study of contact between surfaces resulting in friction and wear.

○ Tribology has been defined as the science and practice of interacting surfaces in relative motion.

○ In tribology, scoring is a severe form of wear characterized by the formation of extensive grooves in the direction of sliding.

---

truss /trʌs/ (trusses)

MECHANICS AND DYNAMICS

NOUN A **truss** is a structure consisting of parts that are either in compression or in tension.

○ The bridge consisted of two trusses with a bridge deck between them.

○ A truss is a structure comprising two types of structural element: compression members and tension members (struts and ties).

---

tun|ing /tunɪŋ/

CONTROL, INSTRUMENTATION AND METROLOGY

NOUN **Tuning** is the adjustment of control parameters so that a system operates in the best possible way.

○ Engine tuning involves modifying automobile engines to improve their performance.

○ Tedious manual tuning is no longer an inevitable part of control systems.

tur|bine /tɜrbɪn/ (turbines)

FLUID ENGINEERING

NOUN A **turbine** is a machine that works by the action of a fluid on a series of surfaces, usually a circular set of blades.

○ In a turbine, moving fluid acts on the blades so that they move and impart rotational energy to the rotor.

○ The steam spins turbines connected to generators to make electricity.

tur|bu|lent /tɜrbyələnt/

FLUID ENGINEERING

ADJECTIVE A **turbulent** flow is a flow in which a fluid moves around in an irregular way.

○ If the valve is opened too far, the flow in the pipe becomes turbulent.

○ In a turbulent flow, there is plenty of energy for mixing to occur.

turn|ing /tɜrnɪŋ/

MANUFACTURING AND ASSEMBLY

NOUN **Turning** is a metal cutting process done on a lathe.

○ A mandrel is a shaft that holds workpieces in place for turning on a lathe.

○ Milling and lathe turning are commonly used machining processes.

t

Uu

u|ni|ax|i|al /yuniæksɪəl/

MECHANICS AND DYNAMICS

ADJECTIVE A **uniaxial** stress or force acts in one direction only.

- Metals are tested under uniaxial stress.
- When a specimen is subjected to a uniaxial loading (along its primary axis) the force acting over the cross-sectional area generates a tensile stress and strain within the material.

u|nit /yunɪt/ (units)

GENERAL

NOUN A **unit** is a mechanical part or set of parts that performs a function within a larger system.

- The hydraulic jacks have an integral pumping unit.
- In this setup, the gearbox, clutch, final drive, and differential are combined into a single unit connected directly to the driveshaft.

u|ni|ver|sal joint /yunɪvɜrsəl dʒɔɪnt/ (universal joints)

GENERAL

NOUN A **universal joint** is a joint between two rotating shafts that allows them to move at any angle and in all directions.

- A universal joint allows the wheel to be steered while still being attached to the drive shaft.
- Universal joints fitted at each end of the propeller shaft allow it to move through an angle while maintaining free rotation.

U

Vv

vac|u|um mold|ing (BRIT **vacuum moulding**) /vækyum mouldɪŋ/

NOUN **Vacuum molding** is a type of molding in which pressure is applied by introducing a vacuum on the side of the mold.

○ *The shells of the hand-held electric drills were produced by vacuum molding.*

○ *In vacuum molding, a vacuum is used to hold the sand in the desired mold shape while the metal is poured in and allowed to solidify.*

> **RELATED WORDS**
>
> Compare **vacuum molding** with **blow molding** in which melted plastic is put in a mold, and then shaped by having compressed air blown into it.

valve /vælv/ (**valves**)

NOUN A **valve** is a device that shuts off, starts, or controls the flow of a fluid.

○ *A simple type of valve consists of a hinged flap that drops to block fluid flow in one direction but is pushed open by flow in the other direction.*

○ *When the steam pressure reaches 15 psi, the safety valve opens and excess steam escapes.*

valve spring /vælv sprɪŋ/ (**valve springs**)

FLUID ENGINEERING

NOUN A **valve spring** is a spring that closes a valve after it has been opened mechanically or by flow pressure.

○ If a valve spring gets worn it loses its pressure and is unable to fully close the valve.

○ If an engine spins too quickly, valve springs cannot act quickly enough to close the valves.

ve|lo|ci|met|ry /vɪləʊsɪmɪtri/

CONTROL, INSTRUMENTATION AND METROLOGY

NOUN **Velocimetry** is the measurement of the flow of a fluid by tracking particles introduced into the flow.

○ The study of the speed of liquids and gases is called velocimetry.

○ Particle velocimetry is when particles are introduced into a flow of water and their speed is measured.

vi|bra|tion /vaɪbreɪʃ°n/

MECHANICS AND DYNAMICS

NOUN **Vibration** is the backward and forward movement of a body.

○ Sound is caused by vibration that makes particles in the air form sound waves.

○ A damper is used to reduce vibration.

vis|co|e|las|tic /vɪskəʊɪlæstɪk/

MECHANICS AND DYNAMICS

ADJECTIVE A **viscoelastic** substance changes shape when a stress is put on it and goes back to its original state when the stress is removed after a period of time.

○ Polypropylene and gelatin are examples of viscoelastic materials.

○ Unlike purely elastic substances, a viscoelastic substance has an elastic component and a viscous component.

V

vis|cos|i|ty /vɪskɒsɪti/

FLUID ENGINEERING

NOUN The **viscosity** of a particular fluid is how easily it flows.

○ Long stringy molecules may have a high viscosity because the molecules can become tangled, which prevents them from flowing.

○ Viscosity is a measure of flowability at particular temperatures.

V

Ww

wash|er /wɒʃər/ (washers)

GENERAL

NOUN A **washer** is a flat ring of metal put under the head of a bolt or nut to spread the load when the bolt or nut is tightened.

○ Put washers under the bolts to prevent damage to the surface being fixed.

○ If a faucet is dripping, you need to replace the washer.

wear /wɛər/

MATERIALS

NOUN **Wear** is a process in which material is gradually removed from one or more surfaces that are in contact.

○ Dust works its way into the bearings and cylinder, causing unnecessary wear.

○ The main purpose of lubricants is to reduce wear of rubbing parts.

web /wɛb/ (webs)

GENERAL

NOUN The **web** of an I-beam or H-beam is the central section that joins the two flanges.

○ The web of the I-beam carries relatively little stress and can therefore be made quite thin.

○ The H-beam has a web that connects a pair of flanges.

wedge /wɛdʒ/ (wedges)

GENERAL

NOUN A **wedge** is a triangular-shaped solid inserted between two parts in order to prevent movement between them or to force them apart.

○ Drive a triangular wedge into the gap to keep the two parts separate.

○ A tapered metal wedge was slid between the flat face of one bar and the curved face of the next.

---

weld|a|bil|i|ty /wɛldəbɪlɪti/

MANUFACTURING AND ASSEMBLY

NOUN The **weldability** of a metal is how easily it can be welded.

○ The criteria in deciding on the weldability of a metal are the weld quality and the ease with which it can be obtained.

○ These alloys have good weldability because they are insensitive to heat treatment.

---

weld|ing /wɛldɪŋ/

MANUFACTURING AND ASSEMBLY

NOUN **Welding** is the process of joining two plastic or metal parts by melting them, with or without using a further molten material.

○ The heat produced by an arc is used in welding to melt metal rods, which solidify to provide a strong joint between two metal surfaces.

○ Special helmets must be worn when doing welding to protect the eyes.

> **RELATED WORDS**
>
> Compare **welding** with **spot-weld**, which is the joining of two pieces of metal by melting small circular areas on the metal using heat from an electric current and applying pressure.

---

wind tur|bine /wɪnd tɜrbɪn/ (**wind turbines**)

ENERGY, THERMODYNAMICS AND HEAT TRANSFER

NOUN A **wind turbine** is a type of electric power generator, in which a shaft is made to rotate by the flow of wind over a propeller.

○ Wind turbines convert wind energy to electricity.

○ Large, modern wind turbines operate together in wind farms to produce electricity for utilities.

w

wing nut /wɪŋ nʌt/ (**wing nuts**)

NOUN A **wing nut** is a threaded nut that you tighten by hand by means of two flat parts projecting from the central body.

○ Wing nuts are used on all of our products because they are assembled by customers who may not have access to tools.

○ Wing nuts are designed to be used where the desired amount of tightness can be obtained by the fingers.

work /wɜrk/

NOUN **Work** is a type of energy associated with a force acting on a large object in order to accelerate it.

○ The work done in compressing the spring is equal to the force times the distance through which it acts.

○ The heated gas expands against a piston doing mechanical work.

work|a|bil|i|ty /wɜrkəbɪlɪti/

NOUN The **workability** of a substance, especially a metal, is how easily it can be changed into a new shape.

○ The workability of a metal can usually be improved by increasing its temperature.

○ The key to producing high-quality decorative concrete is to keep the water-cement ratio as low as possible without sacrificing workability.

work|piece /wɜrkpis/ (**workpieces**)

NOUN A **workpiece** is a piece of raw material that is in the process of being formed into a component or part.

○ Boring fixtures are used to hold the workpiece while it is being bored.

○ Turning is a machining process in which a workpiece is held and rotated against a single-point tool.

worm gear /wɜːm ɡɪər/ (**worm gears**)

MACHINERY AND COMPONENTS

NOUN A **worm gear** is a device consisting of a threaded shaft (a worm) that mates with a gearwheel (the worm wheel), so that rotary motion can be transferred between two shafts at right angles to each other.

○ In worm gears, as the worm revolves, the wormwheel also revolves but the rotary motion is transmitted through a 90 degree angle.

○ Worm gears are used to transmit motion or power between right-angled shafts when a high-ratio reduction is necessary.

---

wrist pin (In BRIT use **gudgeon pin**) /rɪst pɪn/ (**wrist pins**)

MACHINERY AND COMPONENTS

NOUN A **wrist pin** is a pin through the skirt of a piston in an internal-combustion engine, to which the little end of the connecting rod is attached.

○ The bearing at the other end of the connecting rod is known as the little end and holds the wrist pin that is mounted in the piston.

○ The wrist pin connects the piston head to the connecting rod.

W

Yy

yield strength /yi̱ld strɛŋkθ/

MATERIALS

NOUN The **yield strength** of a bar of material is the maximum stress that can be applied along its axis before it begins to change shape.

- o Steel yield strength is the amount of stress a piece of steel must undergo in order to permanently deform.
- o A metal that has a high yield strength can withstand high stress without permanent deformation.

Young's mod|u|lus /yʌŋz mɒdʒələs/

MATERIALS

NOUN The **Young's modulus** is a measure of how stiff a bar of material is along its axis. It is equal to the stress applied divided by the resulting elastic strain. This term is named for English scientist Thomas Young (1773–1829).

- o If the Young's modulus is large, the material will not shrink as much when it is compressed.
- o Young's modulus characterizes how difficult it is to stretch a substance in an elastic way.

> **RELATED WORDS**
>
> Compare **Young's modulus** with the following phrases:
>
> **modulus of elasticity**
> a measure of the stiffness of a material. It is equal to the stress applied to it, divided by the resulting elastic strain.
>
> **shear modulus**
> a measure of the stiffness or rigidity of a material. It is equal to the shear stress divided by the shear strain.

Practice
and
Solutions

1. **Match the device or instrument with the function.**

1	accelerometer	a	measures pressure differences between different points in a fluid
2	interferometer	b	measures how fast a fluid is flowing by recording the pressure decrease across a hole
3	manometer	c	measures components very exactly
4	micrometer	d	measures temperature by means of an expanding column of fluid
5	orifice meter	e	measures distance by seeing how light waves combine
6	thermometer	f	measures the rate at which the velocity of a vibrating object changes

2. **In each set, find the words or phrases that do not exist.**

1 types of gear ....
   a bevel gear   b monkey gear   c spur gear   d worm gear

2 types of casting ....
   a setpoint casting   b die casting   c sand casting
   d investment casting

3 types of joint ....
   a ball-and-socket joint   b knuckle joint   c universal joint
   d slaq joint

4 types of cutting and shaping processes ....
  a seething **b** honing **c** shaping **d** turning

5 types of problems that may occur with metal ....
  a galvanic corrosion **b** cold shuts **c** fracture **d** blots

3. Complete the sentences by writing one word in each gap.

corrosion	friction	air-conditioning
shrinkage	adhesive	condensation

1 You just need a little .... to stick those two parts together.

2 There was .... on the bus so we all kept nice and cool.

3 I had to wipe the .... off the windows because I couldn't see out.

4 The exposed metal surfaces have to be treated in order to prevent ....

5 A little lubrication between moving parts will prevent ....

6 As a plastic material cools, ... occurs.

4. **Match these adjectives with the types of flow that they describe.**

1	turbulent	**a**	describes a heat or mass flow which is even, in which heat or mass does not gather in a particular area
2	inviscid	**b**	describes a flow that does not contain vortices
3	laminar	**c**	describes a type of flow in which viscous forces are very small in comparison with inertial ones
4	steady-state	**d**	describes a flow in which a fluid moves around in an irregular way
5	irrotational	**e**	describes a flow that takes place in layers without interaction between them, so that all parts move in one direction

5. **Choose the correct verb to fill each gap.**

atomized	**drawn**	**meshed**

1 If a liquid fuel is ...., it is made into a fine spray so that it will burn more easily.

tapped	**blanked**	**packed**

2 If a piece of metal is ...., it is stamped, punched, or cut out so that is ready for forging.

bleed	**draw**	**hunt**

3 If you .... a container or an enclosed system, you remove liquid or gas from it.

> idles   fatigues   chatters

4 If a machine part ...., it makes contact with a workpiece in an intermittent way, often causing damage to the workpiece.

> chatters   idles   blanks

5 If an engine or shaft ...., it turns without doing anything useful, for example moving a vehicle forward or making another part move.

> regulates   transmits   registers

6 If a mechanical part ...., it lines up with another.

6. For each question, choose the correct answer.

1 The study of how moving objects behave is called ....
a statics **b** dynamics **c** metrology

2 The study of the transfer and conversion of energy is called ....
a rheology **b** particle kinetics **c** thermodynamics

3 The study of the movement of objects or of groups of objects is called ....
a kinematics **b** statics **c** tribology

4 The study of the flow of liquids which do not flow easily is called ....
a tribology **b** rheology **c** metrology

5 The study of the movement of particles, without considering the forces that cause this movement is called ....
   a particle kinematics   **b** particle kinetics   **c** tribology

6 The study of contact between surfaces resulting in friction and wear is called ....
   a tribology   **b** metallurgy   **c** metrology

7. Which sentences are correct?

1 An adaptive system can change its parameters as the conditions change. ....

2 A floating part or workpiece is making contact with another part. ....

3 Incompressible fluids and solids change in volume if a pressure is applied to them. ....

4 A male component has a hollow part so that the projecting parts on another component fit into it. ....

5 A relieved component has part of its surface cut away to avoid friction or wear. ....

6 Supersonic is used to describe things that move faster than the speed of sound in a particular medium, usually the air. ....

8. Rearrange the letters to find words. Use the definitions to help you.

1 **catautor** ....
(a machine or part of a machine that moves or controls another part in response to an input)

2 **vogreron** ....
(a device that controls the speed of an engine)

3 **ulpimanator** ....
(type of actuator that is used to move objects in a similar way to a human hand)

4 **rorelugat** ....
(a mechanism or device that controls something such as pressure, temperature, or fluid flow)

5 **resosn** ....
(an instrument for detecting a quantity or quality, for example temperature or motion, and returning an electrical output)

6 **ned torfecef** ....
(the part of an actuator that comes into contact with the object being moved or controlled)

9. Put the correct word in each gap.

| poppet | crankshaft | cylinder | crankcase | tappet | sump |

1 .... the metal housing around the crankshaft, connecting rods, etc., in an internal-combustion engine

2 .... a container, such as the lower part of the crankcase of an internal-combustion engine, into which liquids can drain and be used again

3 .... a mushroom-shaped valve often used as an exhaust or inlet valve in an internal-combustion engine

4 .... the part of an internal-combustion engine that transmits motion from the camshaft to the push rods or valves

5 .... a cavity of circular cross-section that contains a moving piston, for example in an internal combustion engine

6 .... the main revolving rod of an internal-combustion engine to which the connecting rods are attached

PRACTICE PRACTICE PRACTICE PRACTICE PRACTICE PRACTICE

10. Choose the correct phrase to fill each gap.

| A crosshead | A shim | A slab |

1 .... is a block between the piston and the connecting rod of an engine, which prevents the piston from moving from side to side and causing damage.

| A centroid | A flywheel | A grinding wheel |

2 .... is a revolving circular object that makes an engine move smoothly by storing kinetic energy and keeping the engine at a constant speed throughout its cycle.

| An air-intake | A port | A socket |

3 .... is an opening through which air enters an engine or system, usually for combustion or cooling.

| A clutch | A dashpot | A throttle |

4 .... is a device that controls the quantity of fuel or fuel and air mixture entering an engine.

| A cylinder | A wrist pin | A poppet |

5 .... is a thin part through the skirt of a piston in an internal-combustion engine, to which the little end of the connecting rod is attached.

| A crankcase | A crankshaft | A camshaft |

6 .... is a rotating rod with one or more projections attached to it, especially one that operates the valves in an internal-combustion engine.

11. Match the two parts together.

1	combustion	a	a nuclear reaction in which energy is produced when atoms split apart
2	condensation	b	the flow of heat from one surface to another by infrared waves
3	excitation	c	the twisting of a part by applying equal and opposite torques at either end
4	fission	d	the process in which a fuel burns in oxygen
5	radiation	e	the act of making something vibrate
6	torsion	f	the process in which a vapor touches a cool surface and turns into a liquid

12. Which sentences are correct?

1 A baffle is a thin flat object that is hung in a flow of liquid or gas to cause partial obstruction. ....

2 A bore is a pipe or duct up which a fluid flows. ....

3 A bypass is a way of diverting a flow of fluid around a system. ....

4 A boiler is a container in which a liquid, usually water, is heated until it changes into a vapor. ....

5 Melting is the action of changing from a solid to a liquid as the temperature is raised. ....

6 A hose is used for carrying liquids only. ....

13. Find the words or phrases that do not belong.

1 Things connected with measuring ....
  a strain gage **b** Pitot tube **c** instrumentation **d** arbor

2 Things connected with gears ....
  a cog **b** differential **c** caliper **d** backlash

3 Things connected with controlling or stopping a flow of fluid
  ....
  a choke **b** stud **c** gate valve **d** cut-off

4 Things connected with the flow of heat ....
  a web **b** radiation **c** conduction **d** fin

5 Things connected with preventing friction ....
  a bearing **b** tappet **c** lubrication **d** bush

14. Rearrange the letters to find words. Use the definitions to help you.

1 **nigdelw** ....
  (the process of joining two plastic or metal parts by melting them,
  with or without using an additional molten material)

2 **oht ingkrow** ....
  (a process in which a metal is shaped under pressure at a fairly high
  temperature)

3 **gorfgin** ....
  (the process of shaping metal into its finished shape by pressing or
  hitting it against an anvil or die)

4 **ningurt** ....
  (a metal cutting process done on a lathe)

5 **glodinm** ....
(a process in which a molten or liquid material is poured into a shape and allowed to set or freeze)

6 **dirnligl** ....
(the process of cutting holes in a solid material using a rotating cutting tool)

15. For each question, choose the correct answer.

1 The use of supports that absorb vibrations to reduce the vibrations that are transmitted to or from a machine or structure is called ....

a isolation **b** excitation **c** condensation

2 The rate at which velocity changes is called ....
a vibration **b** acceleration **c** insulation

3 When a material changes shape when a stress is applied to it but goes back to its original state when the stress is removed, this is called ....

a lubrication **b** plastic deformation **c** elastic deformation

4 The adding of a substance between solid surfaces that are moving against each other in order to reduce friction and wear is called ....

a radiation **b** lubrication **c** rotation

5 When a material changes shape when a stress is applied to it and does not go back to its original state when the stress is removed, this is called ....
a plastic deformation **b** elastic deformation **c** refrigeration

6 The movement of a body around a center is called ....
a consensation **b** free vibration **c** rotation

16. Put the correct word or phrase in each gap.

| mechanical advantage | Young's modulus | stress |
| head | modulus of elasticity | strain |

1 .... a measure of pressure, which is based on the height of a column of liquid

2 .... a measure of a material's stiffness

3 .... a measure of how much a material changes shape under a force

4 .... a measure of the internal forces in a material that changes shape under a force

5 .... a measure of how much a force is increased by using a tool or machine

6 .... a measure of how stiff a bar of material is along its axis

17. Match the two parts together.

1	The workability of a substance, especially a metal,	a	is how easily it can be hardened when cooled rapidly from a high temperature.
2	The efficiency of a process	b	is how easily it can be made to operate at a setpoint without fluctuating.
3	The hardenability of steel		
4	The hardness of a material	c	is how strong or resistant to wear it is.
5	The machinability of a material	d	is how easily it can be shaped or cut using a tool.
		e	is how near it is to being perfect.
6	The stability of a control system	f	is how easily it can be changed into a new shape.

18. Put each sentence into the correct order.

1 worked on / as part of / the assembly line / of the factory / my training I

....

....

2 point at / the boiling / a hundred degrees / water reaches / Celsius

....

....

3 for bicycle / less brittle / is widely used / frames because it is / this metal

....

....

4 fumes is / air pollution / potentially very / dangerous / from exhaust

....

....

5 metal / cause of / most likely / the crash / fatigue was the

....

....

6 robots are / nowadays most / used in / operations / manufacturing

....

....

19. Rearrange the letters to find words. Use the definitions to help you.

1 **loracl** ....

(a ring or tube that fits onto a shaft or rod, for example to prevent a part from coming off the end of a shaft)

2 **gaec** ....

(a device that fits into a rolling bearing and keeps the right amount of space between its individual rollers or balls)

3 **hicp** ....

(a small piece of material that comes off the surface of a workpiece when it is being cut)

4 **tekags** ....

(a piece of paper, rubber, or other material that can be pressed between the faces or flanges of a joint to provide a seal)

5 **cajkte** ....

(a cover or casing for the outside of something, for example the insulating cover of a boiler)

6 **lanjuro** ....

(the part of a shaft or axle that is in contact with or enclosed by a bearing)

PRACTICE PRACTICE PRACTICE PRACTICE PRACTICE

20. Put the correct word or phrase in each gap.

shear force	distributed force	impact
thrust	drag	centrifugal force

1 .... the tendency of an object moving in a circle to travel away from the center of the circle

2 .... the force that a fluid exerts on an object caused by a difference in velocity between the fluid and the object

3 .... the force that makes one surface of a substance move over another parallel surface

4 .... pressure that is exerted continuously by one object against another, especially the axial force by or on a shaft

5 .... a force that acts on a large part of a surface, not just on one place

6 .... the sudden application of a force

Solutions

Exercise 1
1. **f** measures the rate at which the velocity of a vibrating object changes
2. **e** measures distance by seeing how light waves combine
3. **a** measures pressure differences between different points in a fluid
4. **c** measures components very exactly
5. **b** measures how fast a fluid is flowing by recording the pressure decrease across a hole
6. **d** measures temperature by means of an expanding column of fluid

Exercise 2
1. **b** monkey gear
2. **a** setpoint casting
3. **d** slag joint
4. **a** seething
5. **d** blots

Exercise 3
1. adhesive
2. air-conditioning
3. condensation
4. corrosion
5. friction
6. shrinkage

Exercise 4
1. **d** describes a flow in which a fluid moves around in an irregular way
2. **c** describes a type of flow in which viscous forces are very small in comparison with inertial ones
3. **e** describes a flow that takes place in layers without interaction between them, so that all parts move in one direction
4. **a** describes a heat or mass flow which is even, in which heat or mass does not gather in a particular area
5. **b** describes a flow that does not contain vortices

Exercise 5
1. atomized
2. blanked
3. bleed
4. chatters
5. idles
6. registers

Exercise 6
1. **b** dynamics
2. **c** thermodynamics
3. **a** kinematics
4. **b** rheology
5. **a** particle kinematics
6. **a** tribology

Exercise 7
1. An adaptive system can change its parameters as the conditions change.
5. A relieved component has part of its surface cut away to avoid friction or wear.
6. Supersonic is used to describe things that move faster than the speed of sound in a particular medium, usually the air.

Exercise 8
1. actuator
2. governor
3. manipulator
4. regulator
5. sensor
6. end effector

Exercise 9
1. crankcase
2. sump
3. poppet
4. tappet
5. cylinder
6. crankshaft

Exercise 10
1. A crosshead
2. A flywheel
3. An air-intake
4. A throttle
5. A wrist pin
6. A camshaft

Exercise 11

1 **d** the process in which a fuel burns in oxygen
2 **f** the process in which a vapor touches a cool surface and turns into a liquid
3 **e** the act of making something vibrate
4 **a** a nuclear reaction in which energy is produced when atoms split apart
5 **b** the flow of heat from one surface to another by infrared waves
6 **c** the twisting of a part by applying equal and opposite torques at either end

Exercise 12

1 A baffle is a thin flat object that is hung in a flow of liquid or gas to cause partial obstruction.
3 A bypass is a way of diverting a flow of fluid around a system.
4 A boiler is a container in which a liquid, usually water, is heated until it changes into a vapour.
5 Melting is the action of changing from a solid to a liquid as the temperature is raised.

Exercise 13

1 **d** arbor
2 **c** caliper
3 **b** stud
4 **a** web
5 **b** tappet

Exercise 14

1 welding
2 hot working
3 forging
4 turning
5 molding
6 drilling

Exercise 15

1 **a** isolation
2 **b** acceleration
3 **c** elastic deformation
4 **b** lubrication
5 **a** plastic deformation
6 **c** rotation

Exercise 16

1 head
2 modulus of elasticity
3 strain
4 stress
5 mechanical advantage
6 Young's modulus

Exercise 17

1 **f** is how easily it can be changed into a new shape.
2 **e** is how near it is to being perfect.
3 **a** is how easily it can be hardened when cooled rapidly from a high temperature.
4 **c** is how strong or resistant to wear it is.
5 **d** is how easily it can be shaped or cut using a tool.
6 **b** is how easily it can be made to operate at a setpoint without fluctuating.

Exercise 18

1 as part of my training I worked on the assembly line of the factory
2 water reaches the boiling point at a hundred degrees Celsius
3 this metal is widely used for bicycle frames because it is less brittle
4 air pollution from exhaust fumes is potentially very dangerous
5 metal fatigue was the most likely cause of the crash
6 nowadays most robots are used in manufacturing operations

Exercise 19

1 collar
2 cage
3 chip
4 gasket
5 jacket
6 journal

Exercise 20

1 centrifugal force
2 drag
3 shear force
4 thrust
5 distributed force
6 impact

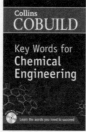
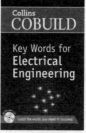

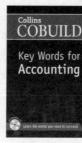

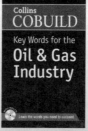